Showing to Win

Showing to Win

Carolyn Henderson
and
Lynn Russell

SWAN·HILL
PRESS

DEDICATION
This book is in memory of Cosmic, a great show cob and a
great character, who died just after it was completed.

Copyright © 1993 by Carolyn Henderson

First published in the UK in 1993
by Swan Hill Press
an imprint of Airlife Publishing Ltd.

Reprinted 1994

British Library Cataloguing in Publication Data
   A catalogue record for this book
   is available from the British Library

ISBN 1 85310 389 6

Printed by Livesey Ltd, Shrewsbury.

Swan Hill Press
an imprint of Airlife Publishing Ltd.
101 Longden Road, Shrewsbury SY3 9EB

Contents

Introduction

Showing is becoming more popular every year, and whatever type of horse you own, you will have no problems finding suitable shows to enter. In fact, you will be spoilt for choice – there were at least 7,000 shows advertised nationally this year, and they formed just the tip of the iceberg. Add the ones that are only of 'local' interest and you can see that showing is enjoying a real boom in popularity.

If each of those 7,000 shows hold six showing classes, you have 42,000 chances of catching the judges' eye. But as most showing classes attract at least 15 entrants, often more, plenty of other people will be trying to do the same thing. That is where this book comes in: there is no magic wand that can transform an average horse into a Wembley winner, but there are plenty of ways to make sure that the odds of heading a final line-up are in your favour.

For most showing enthusiasts, cantering a lap of honour under the Wembley spotlights is the ultimate dream. It is very rare for that dream to come true for an amateur rider, but it has been known . . . and there is no reason why it should not happen again. Whether your aim is to produce a champion of champions or to win your class at your riding club's summer show, the ingredients for success are the same. New classes have recently been introduced for amateur riders of show hunters, culminating in a final at the Royal International Horse Show. Add these to cob classes for amateur rider/owners and special awards for amateurs that are given in many other sections, and you have plenty of scope for glory.

At the big shows (county level and above) the prizes inevitably go to professionals. Stand at the ringside while the judge makes his or her final decision and you will often hear someone comment 'My horse is as nice as that one!' That may well be true, but the nicest horse in the world still has to be prepared, produced and ridden to the highest standards if its worth is to be recognised.

You do not have to be a professional to win. You do need to have professional standards, though, plus other essentials like time, dedication, skill and – to a certain extent – money. Finding the time means reorganising your life, which can be difficult (but not impossible) if you have a job and/or a family to take into consideration. Dedication is something that makes you carry on when you have to get up at six in the morning and it is cold, dark and pouring with rain. Skills can be learned, as can making the most of your money by investing it in good quality essentials, whether they be lessons with a showing professional or tack that enhances your horse's conformation.

If you have unlimited time and money, you can happily go off and buy your perfectly schooled, county standard show hunter, kit it and yourself out from the top shops and expect to do well. Most of us do not have those advantages, and have to work within a tight budget. We have to make success rather than buy it – and the nice thing is that this kind of success can be much more enjoyable.

One of the first things you have to decide is whether you want to buy a horse specifically for showing, or make the most of the one you already have. If you are content to show at local level and your horse has reasonable conformation and is (or will be!) well schooled, there is no reason why you should not do well. But if you are determined to win at county level or even beyond, you must have the horsepower to do it. And unless you are very lucky, that means spending a lot of money.

There are all sorts of stories about people buying an ex-racehorse for under £1,000 and turning it into a top show hack. There are even more cases of people buying hopefully and finding that their ugly ducklings do not turn into swans, after all! If you have a good eye for a horse and a lot of luck, you may find a bargain: but remember that there are many other people trying to do the same, and a large percentage of them are professionals who do it for a living.

Professional showing people, who are competing most weekends throughout the season, usually restrict their show horses to that particular job and keep them sweet at home through a mixture of hacking out, schooling and turning out. But a horse that is successful in the show ring can be equally successful in other spheres, particularly in the hands of an owner who shows for fun rather than as a living.

For instance, a nice cob is the ultimate all-rounder; he can do all riding club activities, from dressage to show jumping, and will give you a nice hack and probably a good day's hunting. Likewise, a hunter or riding horse should be able to turn his hoof to most things.

If you are planning to do some reasonably serious showing, you also need to consider the facilities that are available to you. Again, there have been cases of talented riders schooling horses to a high standard just when hacking round the roads – but they are few and far between. It is not necessary to have the luxury of an indoor school available, but you do need at least a level area where you can work your horse.

Producing a show horse is a bit like doing a jigsaw, which is where much of its fascination lies. Skills such as feeding, clipping and trimming, schooling and turnout come together to form an overall picture. One person must be in charge of creating that picture: you. By all means get help and advice, but remember that it is ultimately down to you. You must be able to assess your horse and make any adjustments necessary to his management.

For instance, if he seems lethargic or over the top, you may need to adjust his diet. If he is resistant when you ride him, you need to decide whether he needs more schooling, or whether you have overdone it and he needs a change of scene to get him happy and co-operative again. All this means that you need to be in total control of his lifestyle, and if you have to keep him at livery that might not always be possible.

Some yards are excellent and will co-operate in as many ways as they can, but others cannot or will not co-operate with the finely tuned routine that a show horse needs. It can be a problem if you are the odd one out: for instance, if you are the only showing enthusiast in a yard run for eventers, by an eventer. Their goals are so different that you may well end up with a lean, super-fit horse instead of a well-covered show animal that gives a mannered ride.

So before you even start reading the show schedules, look at what you have now – your horse, your yard, your budget and your lifestyle. Decide what, if anything, you need to change and whether or not you are able or prepared to do it: this could mean anything from changing yards to selling your present horse and looking for another. You should be left with a clear idea of the showing opportunities open to you.

Chapter 1
Choice of Horse

Successful showing is very much a matter of horses for courses. It is not enough to have an animal that has good conformation and movement, presence, a nice temperament and gives the judge a wonderful ride – though you should, of course, count your blessings if you own such a paragon! On top of all this, a show horse must be what is called true to type; in other words, he must fit into a definite category.

The higher the level you compete at, the more important this is. At riding club level, it is not unknown for a horse to be placed in, say, riding horse and working hunter classes. At county level, this would be unlikely because the two are different types and the judges would be looking for different qualities – though having said that, people do sometimes show the same horse in different categories even though it is not strictly correct. Read the schedules carefully; standards are getting higher all the time at smaller shows, and many now say that horses can be entered in one category but not in another.

It can be very hard to stand back and assess your horse dispassionately, especially if he (or she) is part of the family and you get a lot of fun and enjoyment out of him. But this is essential if you want to get your showing career off on the right hoof, and one of the best ways is to visit a few shows and see the wide variety of classes available and what the judges seem to like and dislike. If you are buying a horse to show, ringside viewing (combined with a spot of ringside judging as you get more confident) is also a good way of deciding what type of animal would suit you most.

Some classes tend to offer more scope for the amateur than others . . . though the word 'amateur' is not used in any derogatory fashion. It is merely the best way of defining someone who does not show for a living, as is the case with a professional. Having said that, at larger shows you will be up against the professionals in all classes – and you are also likely to find them introducing their young, novice horses to the showring atmosphere at smaller ones early in the season.

Look at any schedule and you will see that hunter classes (the weight divisions) are given the prime time, the best ring and the best prize money – though you will never get rich on prize money. Show jumpers might win thousands throughout the season, but even the top show horses can count their winnings in hundreds. Professionals make their living with the help of sponsorship and/or showing for owners who pay the bills, and usually through sidelines such as buying and selling, schooling and teaching.

This means that sponsoring companies, who want their names to get as much publicity as possible, inevitably go for hunters. In turn, this makes the top quality horses very expensive, unless you have the knowledge and luck to find a promising youngster before anyone else (usually a professional!) spots its potential.

Cobs, small hunters, working hunters, riding horses and to a certain extent hacks are usually a more realistic proposition. The cob is the ultimate family horse, though a top class show cob who can take on the professionals in the weight classes can easily set you back £5,000 to £10,000-plus. But there are also classes specifically for amateur owner/riders, judged as showing classes, and for working cobs, where you will be asked to jump a course of natural fences.

If you are a one or two-horse owner, you probably want an animal that will also give you a lot fun in other activities. Out of season, a cob will hunt, jump, hack, do sponsored rides, dressage . . . in fact, anything you want him to. There have been cases of show cobs competing in dressage at Grand Prix level; they do not have the movement to compete with the extravagance of a warmblood or Thoroughbred, but they do not disgrace themselves. In the same way, a nice quality riding horse can be a mannered hack, a good bet for dressage and a competent jumper, giving you a very classy all-rounder.

Whatever job you buy a horse for, he must suit your pocket, your personality and your riding ability. Do not be tempted to over-horse yourself just because you think a big horse looks impressive. You will often see small professionals, usually women, on 17hh horses in the show ring – but behind that polished performance lie years of experience and hours of schooling at home. If you are generously proportioned, the cob comes in to his own: a heavyweight cob can carry 14 stone and over, and a well-made horse will be deep enough through the girth to accommodate the most long-legged rider.

Heights can be deceptive. People often think that successful show horses are bigger than they are, and assume that the owner has taught them to bend at the knees to get that all-important height certificate. In fact, a well-made 15.2hh that 'fills the eye' can give the illusion of being bigger than a 16hh horse with poorer conformation. Do not assume that you cannot buy a small hunter or a cob because you will look too big on it; most riders up to about five feet eight inches look in proportion with a good, up to height 15.2hh – and as for cobs, literally anyone can ride them.

Cobs

The show cob is the ultimate fun horse, and is characterised by his chunky build and hogged mane. He must be over 14.2hh but not exceed 15.1hh and can be lightweight (to carry up to 14 stone) or heavyweight (14 stone and over).

A cob should have 'a head like a duchess and and a backside like a cook.' He needs to be a comfortable ride – with the ability to gallop – and to have lots of presence. A lightweight needs a minimum of eight and a half inches of bone. Bone is measured just below the knee; a lightweight should have eight and a half to nine inches of bone, and a heavyweight should have at least nine inches plus with build in proportion.

A cob is the ultimate fun horse – and must have the ability to gallop, as Lynn Russell and Pluto demonstrate.

Cobs have powerful back ends and are often good jumpers. Working cob classes, similar to those for working hunters, can offer a lot of fun to a rider who enjoys jumping. There are also classes for novice horses and amateur owner/riders: this is the only showing area to offer classes specifically for non-professionals, which just goes to show how popular cobs have become. It is not unusual to find 25 or more in a class at a county show.

It is often said that a good cob is an accident rather than the result of a planned breeding programme, though many have a percentage of Irish Draught or heavy horse blood. The British Show Hack, Cob and Riding Horse Association has just introduced cob breeding classes, which may encourage more people to try and breed this type of horse.

A cob is always workmanlike, but a good one is never common: he still has plenty of quality and must be a good mover in order to be a comfortable ride. Beware the boneshakers with straight shoulders; they may do an excellent job between the shafts, but will not endear themselves to a showing judge.

A show horse must have presence – and the light-weight cob Cosmic had more than his fair share of this 'Look at me' quality.

Hunters

Show hunters are divided into three weight sections: lightweight, to carry up to 12 stone 7lb; middleweight (12 stone 7lb to 14 stone) and heavyweight (14 stone and over). There are also classes for ladies' hunters, to be ridden side-saddle, novices and four-year-olds.

Show hunters are invariably 16.2hh and upwards, though the height should be in proportion to the weight division. A 17.3hh heavyweight can be an imposing animal, but a 17.2hh lightweight could be out of proportion with long, spindly legs. The judge is still looking for a horse that would stay all day in the hunting field, and giraffes are out of place.

If you want to exhibit in the weight categories, you need a horse that belongs in an appropriate category. For instance, a light middleweight (a horse that is just out of lightweights but not far enough along the next weight scale) will never do as well as a true middleweight. However, there is no reason why a horse that does not quite have a true weight cannot do well in ladies' or working hunter classes.

Show hunter classes are the most prestigious on the schedule. Wishful Thinking, successful in lightweight and ladies' classes.

Small hunters can give the amateur owner a lot of fun. They tend to be a low priority for most professionals, because they do not qualify for a championship at one of the big end of season shows such as the Royal International Horse Show and are usually put in a side ring rather than the prestigious main ring at county shows. This makes them cheaper than the 'proper' show hunter, though of course cheapness is only relative!

Working hunter classes give an extra opportunity to the well-made horse of true hunter type who can jump a good round over a course of natural fences. They are open to horses over 15hh and are usually divided into lightweight and heavyweight sections, depending on the size of the show. This can again give another opportunity to a horse who does not quite fit into one of the show hunter weight divisions.

It goes without saying that to do well in working classes, a horse needs to have a good jump and to be well-schooled enough to jump in a flowing style. This is reflected in the way working hunters are judged – 60 per cent of the marks are allocated for jumping

A heavyweight hunter should combine quality and substance. The rider, Ken Spencer, is beautifully turned out.

(performance and style) and 40 per cent for ride and conformation. Working hunter and cob classes are the one division where a horse will not necessarily be penalised for acquired blemishes, such as scars, as it is assumed that they could be 'honourable scars' from the hunting field.

Unfortunately a lot of people think that because their horse is brilliant out hunting or can canter down to a three feet nine inches fence at home, he will automatically do well in working hunter classes. The reality is that even though the fences are of a natural appearance. jumping between eight and twelve in cold blood is very different from jumping in a crowd or popping a decent sized fence or two at home.

There is also the point that course designers' ideas of what constitutes a 'natural' fence can be open to interpretation. It is not unusual to be faced with a bright blue water jump or a one-stride double of gleaming white gates, so make sure your horse is jumping confidently in the ring before entertaining any serious working hunter ambitions. If you are aiming for county level, he should be capable of jumping clear and confidently round a Newcomers course.

So what makes a good show hunter? Basically, he should make the judge feel that he could hunt him all day without having to kick him in the ribs or risk his arms being pulled out. He should be comfortable and forward-going, up to the bridle but not heavy on the hands. He must also really gallop on – but be happy to come back when asked. Too many

A four-year-old potential small hunter.

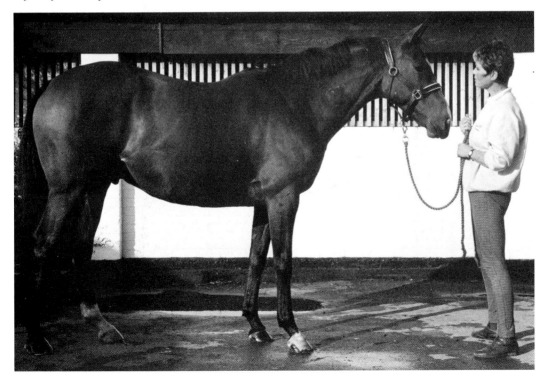

people manage the first but forget the importance of the second; in the hunting field, this could be unforgiveable.

Hacks

The hack is the epitome of elegance – a horse you want to be seen on. Originally he was just that, a horse that ladies and gentlemen could ride in places like Hyde Park to socialise with (and show off to) their friends.

The show hack should be a joy to look at and ride. He must be well mannered, with free flowing movement; he needs to point his toe and not have too much knee action. There is no weight restriction for hacks, but they are basically a lightweight stamp of horse. Having said that, they should not be weeds. The sort of hack that catches the judge's eye will present a balanced outline, with quality limbs and good conformation. His head should be sharp and well set on; a hunter or cob's head will be workmanlike or even a little plain, but a hack should have beauty in every line.

The hack is the epitome of elegance, as Katie Moore demonstrates so beautifully.

Hack classes are divided into small and large divisions. Small hacks are over 14.2hh but not over 15hh, and large hacks are over 15hh but not exceeding 15.3hh. This and the other requirements mean that the best ones are usually Thoroughbreds or Anglo-Arabs, which often mean they are not practical propositions for amateur owners.

Producing a blood horse, especially if he is an ex-racehorse, can be difficult . . . but if you have your heart set on one of these elegant animals and have the time and money to keep him cosseted and well-schooled, do not be put off. Another point which often rules them out is that they are such specialist show animals that they are not versatile enough for most 'ordinary' owners. It might be worth compromising and going for a riding horse, instead.

Riding horses

The riding horse is a cross between the lightweight hunter and the show hack. He is the sort of versatile animal you would be happy to ride at any pace, in any conditions. You are looking for something that has good conformation, is well-schooled and can carry the average adult.

There are two sections: small, for horses exceeding 14.2hh but not over 15.2hh, and large, for 15.2hh and over. Riding horses do not have to jump, but must be able to gallop – you should feel that you could take him for a long ride in the country and be able to cope with whatever comes your way. He should be well-schooled enough to go on and come back whenever you ask; in other words, the sort of quality horse, with the correct bone and substance for his height and type, that you get on and don't want to get off.

When riding horse classes were first introduced they attracted mainly amateur owners, but now you will find a mixture of amateurs and professionals. The very best riding horses are often Thoroughbreds, but (as with hacks) these may be too expensive and/or sharp for the amateur owner. Three-quarter-breds and Anglo-Arabs often do well. A riding horse can be as versatile as a cob, though obviously he will not be up to as much weight.

Coloured horses

Societies such as the Coloured Horse and Pony Society hold their own shows and sponsor classes at others specifically for skewbalds and piebalds. These include classes organised and judged along the same lines as those at other shows, such as riding horse and working hunters.

Breed classes

If your horse or pony is registered with a breed society, you can show him in breed classes for pure or part-breds: see Chapter 2.

Whatever category you decide on, you need a horse that has correct conformation and moves well. But there is another vital ingredient that is just as (if not more) important – temperament. The best-looking, most free-moving horse in the world is no good if he has an unreliable temperament; if he blows up in the ring, he will be put straight down the line, and rightly so.

There are admittedly some top horses with less than perfect temperaments, but you will find that these are all produced by professionals who know how to deal with them. They have the time, experience and facilities that few amateur owners can match; they also do not have to like a horse to do well with it. If your horse is your only horse, you *have* to like him: otherwise the relationship will be as bad as an unhappy marriage! It is often said that opposites attract, but this rarely works with horses and riders. The best combinations are usually those with similar natures – so be honest about your own ability and personality. There is no such thing as right and wrong character traits, because all have their plus and minus points; a bold extrovert does not have to be aggressive, and a quiet, more reserved individual is not necessarily a wimp.

Put a bold rider with a bold horse and you may well get an unbeatable combination, whereas a more cautious partner may not be able to trust this kind of horse and they could well end up losing confidence in each other. A brave rider may give a certain amount of confidence or 'oomph' to a laid-back horse, but in the end this could equally spell disaster. The time is likely to come when either the horse is being pushed beyond its abilities, and decides to say 'No thank you,' or when the rider does not have enough bottle for both of them. The average, reasonably competent rider needs an honest, willing horse who is neither too sharp nor too lazy to take advantage of them.

Personal likes, dislikes and prejudices must also be taken into account. Just as we are not always attracted to or get on with the same sort of person, so we do not all like the same sort of horse. If you cannot stand chestnuts or greys, or feel you could not cope with a mare whose behaviour alters while she is in season, do not buy one! It is no good telling yourself that your prejudice is totally illogical and that a horse's colour is the last thing that you should worry about; if you are going to look over its stable door every morning and think 'You'd be very nice if only you were bay/grey/whatever' you are not exactly sowing the seeds of a promising relationship.

Having said that, it is always best to keep an open mind on sex and colour: in fact, with horses it is best to keep an open mind on everything! 'Strong' colours such as bay and dark brown are undoubtedly safe, but there is another side to the coin. When a judge has fifteen bay hunters cantering round the ring plus a couple of chestnuts or greys, which is he going to notice, albeit unconsciously?

There has even been a lessening in the prejudice against coloured horses in recent years; in fact, they are now so popular they have their own societies, classes and shows. The day has yet to come when a skewbald or piebald wins a show hunter class, but it may happen if the right horse comes up in front of the right, open-minded judge. (Remember that judges are only human, and as such have their own likes and dislikes.) There have, however, been several coloured horses which have done well in working hunter classes.

Many people are reluctant to buy mares, but the fact remains that a good mare is often better than a good gelding. A gelding is, after all, a castrated male that can never have the presence of a stallion; a mare, like a stallion, has had nothing taken away from her and will often have that extra sparkle.

There is also the point that if a gelding has an accident or comes to the end of his showing career, he does not have much of a future. A good mare who has proved herself in competition can be equally successful as a brood mare. These days she does not even have to retire to stud: the advances in embryo transfer techniques allow top mares to be mums and winners at the same time.

You also need to decide whether you are going to look for a youngster to bring on, a horse that knows its job but is still young or a schoolmaster who has left his youth behind but still has a good few years in him. The financial consideration is obviously a major factor, but it must not be the only one. You should only buy a young horse if you have the experience, time and facilities to bring him on, or can afford to pay someone knowledgeable to help you. Having said that, nothing can give greater satisfaction than winning a class and knowing that it is 'all your own work'.

The most expensive horse in terms of the initial purchase is the well-schooled five to eight-year-old who, once you have got to know each other, is ready to go out and do the job. The drawback is that one person's definition of well-schooled may not be the same as yours, and if you are not careful you may find yourself having to sort out behaviour or schooling problems that are not acceptable to you.

Although there is always a market for a good schoolmaster, in general prices tend to drop once a horse is eleven or older. However, if you are new to showing it might be worth considering an older horse: if he knows the job, he will give you the confidence to do it well even if he can never outshine the younger up-and-coming stars. Be careful, though, that you do not buy a horse who is so jaded with showing that he would really rather throw in the towel.

Finding the right show horse is difficult enough – though it is an enjoyable challenge. If you accept the prejudices you feel you cannot change, but keep an open mind on as much as possible, you give yourself the best chance of success.

Chapter 2
The Breeds

It is often said that the British breed some of the best horses in the world, but do not know how to market them. We certainly lag behind the Continentals in the way we keep breeding records, but that situation is starting to change. The old belief that it did not matter how a horse was bred as long as he or she did the job (except, of course, in racing) is being replaced by a growing faith in performance bloodlines.

Bailey's Penarth Blue Steel, a Welsh Cob cross Thoroughbred who has been successful in his first season in middleweight hunter and working hunter classes.

Castle Chieftan, a Thoroughbred cross Irish Draught stallion who has BSJA winnings and is an intermediate eventer. He would make a superb working hunter – but stallions are not allowed to compete in this class.

Many Continentals will not even look at a horse unless they can trace its pedigree back through at least half a dozen generations. We have not reached that situation yet (and hopefully will never get to the stage where the horse with all the qualifications to do a job will be overlooked because of a hazy ancestry) but in sports like show jumping and eventing, proven bloodlines are becoming increasingly more important.

From a showing point of view, it does not matter how a gelding is bred if he has the right qualifications. It is a definite bonus if a mare has papers because when her showing days are over and you want to breed a foal from her, her progeny will be worth that much more. You can also, of course, show her in hand as a broodmare.

Breeding is often very much a matter of fashion, and fashions in horses come and go just as they do in anything else. The most enduring fashion has been the success of the

Irish-bred horse – either Irish Draught cross Thoroughbred or three-quarters Thoroughbred, quarter Irish Draught. As a result you will often see horses advertised for sale that are described as 'Irish' or 'Irish-bred': the claim may well be true, but unless there are registration papers to prove it the horse's ancestry could just as well be a selling point devised by an optimistic owner.

Horses are as much individuals as people, and the way a horse is reared, schooled, fed and managed can have as much effect on his ability and even temperament as does the way he is bred. Having said that, most breeds undoubtedly have characteristics – both good and not so good – that are passed on.

It is often possible to make an informed guess at a horse's parentage just by looking at him, as some breeds have definite characteristics that they usually pass on. The most obvious is the Arab; a dished head and high tail carriage usually means a percentage of Arab blood. The Thoroughbred imparts quality and sensitivity to anything it is crossed with, and work horses such as the Irish Draught add substance and often a dash of common sense.

Cobs are often of indeterminate breeding, but usually have a large percentage of draught or heavy horse blood.

Just as important, different breeds have different personality traits that seem to stay fairly constant, provided the horse has a good environment. (It is often said that there is no such thing as a bad horse: only a bad handler. You could argue that one all day, but there must be some truth in it. Just look at any badly behaved children you know, and watch how their parents deal with them!) So while nothing with horses is ever constant, it is fair to say that if you know how a horse is bred, you can make a reasonably accurate prediction as to his likely plus and minus points.

Remember that horse and pony breeds have been developed by us to do particular jobs. For instance, the Cleveland Bay was originally a carriage horse and still does that job very well; as a result he tends to be straight in the shoulder, because basically that makes it easier for him to pull a load, and upright in the pastern. By crossing a Cleveland with a Thoroughbred you can and often do get a quality riding horse – but he will often have a tendency to be straight in the shoulder and upright, which makes for an up and down action and an uncomfortable ride.

So while you cannot assume that all Arabs will be hot and flighty, all Thoroughbreds will be fast and sharp and all horses with draught-type blood will have poor shoulders, be aware of the prepotency of breed characteristics detailed here. Do not let them put you off going to look at a particular horse, because you might be lucky and find the exception to the rule – but make sure you keep them in mind.

Arabs

The Arab is a breed that you either love or hate. Those who love them say that they are beautiful, independent, intelligent and possessed of great courage and stamina; those who hate them insist that they are hot-headed, flashy and only suitable for racing, endurance riding or very exciting hacks! Prejudice apart, the Arab is the oldest and purest of all the breeds and has had an influence on many of the others.

Most Arabs are between 14.2hh and 15hh, and an Arab is referred to as a horse even when its size decrees that it should be a pony. The most striking conformation points are a finely chiselled, dished head and high tail carriage; these are often passed on, albeit to a lesser extent, when it is crossed with other breeds. They have silky manes and tails that are often sparse, and the usual colours are chestnut, grey, bay and occasionally black.

Although they look fine and delicate, Arabs can in some ways be remarkably tough. They have fine but dense bone, and amazing amounts of stamina – hence their superiority as endurance horses. This stamina sometimes means that they are only happy when given lots of work, which can be a problem for working owners.

Arabs often have a floating action that can be inherited by Anglo or part-bred progeny. This is desirable in a hack, but it would be rare to find a successful part-bred Arab show hunter. If you are looking for a show horse that needs to be elegant, Arab blood can be an advantage: if your competition blueprint demands a workmanlike outlook, it will probably be out of place.

A pure-bred Arab, shown as the rules demand with mane and tail neither pulled nor plaited.

The Arab temperament is a matter for debate. There is no doubt that you will find a lot who are sensitive and boil over very easily, but there are also Arabs who are as sensible as you could wish for. They are usually very much one-man (or woman) horses, who respond best to being cared for and ridden by the same person. This is said to be because they were traditionally kept as part of the tribe and have been bred to have close contact with people.

Anglo and part-bred Arab

Anglos and part-breds often do well in hack and riding horse classes, which demand elegance and quality. An Anglo-Arab is a cross between a Thoroughbred and an Arab; it does not matter which breed provides the stallion and which the mare, though many breeders believe that if you use an Arab stallion on a Thoroughbred mare you are more likely to get bigger stock. For our show classes, a part-bred Arab must have at least 25 per cent Arab blood and the registration papers to prove it.

In theory, the Anglo-Arab combines the best of both worlds. A really good specimen will combine the beauty of both breeds with size, sufficient substance and a temperament that is more equable than either pure-bred. In practice, this is a generalisation that works some, but not all of the time!

In showing terms, an Anglo or part-bred Arab is much more versatile than a pure-bred. It can allow you to compete in breed classes, plus hack or riding horse ones (according to your particular horse's type). Out of the show ring, it can also do well in dressage; it will probably not move as extravagantly, but many have correct paces that make them a comfortable ride. At local level, they often excel in riding club horse classes.

You can argue that there is no reason why a pure-bred Arab cannot fulfil the requirements made by riding horse and hack judges. If you get a good one, this argument can hold true; in fact, the Arab stallion Carrick Crystif, ridden by Lynn Russell, was supreme ridden champion of the 1984 Royal International Horse Show. But the fact remains that these classes have developed along definite lines, and judges have an equally definite ideal pattern of horse.

A versatile part-bred Arab, shown correctly with pulled and plaited mane and pulled tail.

Unfortunately for Arab enthusiasts, their breed does not fit this pattern. Judges look for an understated rather than flashy elegance; Arabs are bred to go with heads and tails in the air and manes and tails flowing as they move. However you describe their appeal, it could never be in terms of understatement or subtlety.

Unless you want to show purely in breed classes, satisfy your admiration of the Arab with an Anglo or part-bred.

Thoroughbred

The Thoroughbred is often described as the perfect horse. It owes a lot to the influence of the Arab, and in turn has itself influenced probably every horse breed in Europe. A good Thoroughbred has everything: quality, substance, beauty, movement and intelligence. The bad news is that there are also plenty of poorer specimens.

You can never get away from the fact that the Thoroughbred is bred for speed. This shows in common conformation points such as length (fine as long as it is in proportion; see Chapter 3 on conformation) and a long, low action. It also accounts for why many top eventers are Thoroughbreds – because they need stamina and the ability to jump at speed – but comparatively few excel as show jumpers or dressage horses. A Thoroughbred will nearly always be bay, brown, chestnut or grey – you will never find a palomino, piebald or skewbald.

A top quality, true middleweight Thoroughbred is the most desirable, and therefore the most expensive, horse you can find. Imagine him as a show hunter: with such quality, substance and galloping ability, what could match him? Middleweight Thoroughbreds are fairly rare, though; most are lightweights and you will find extremely successful hacks and riding horses registered with Weatherbys.*

Some of them will even have come off the racecourse; the 'wastage rate' in racing is around an incredible 75 per cent. This comprises horses that are simply not fast enough, as well as those which do not stand up to training or actual racing. In the right hands, they can be re-schooled.

The good thing about them is that they usually have excellent stable manners and are good in traffic and to load; if they have been racing a few times, they will have seen the sights and will have the experience of an older horse.

Unfortunately there is also a long minus list. Thoroughbreds tend to be sensitive and sharp, simply because of their fine breeding, which can show in all sorts of ways. Whereas a half-bred horse will often warn you by its reactions when it is going to spook or shy, a Thoroughbred can have all four feet off the ground before the average rider realises anything is amiss. Most of them are used to being ridden in strings, and you can have problems when they are first asked to work alone which, if not dealt with properly, can

---

* Weatherbys is the governing body for the *General Stud Book,* in which all Thoroughbreds are registered.

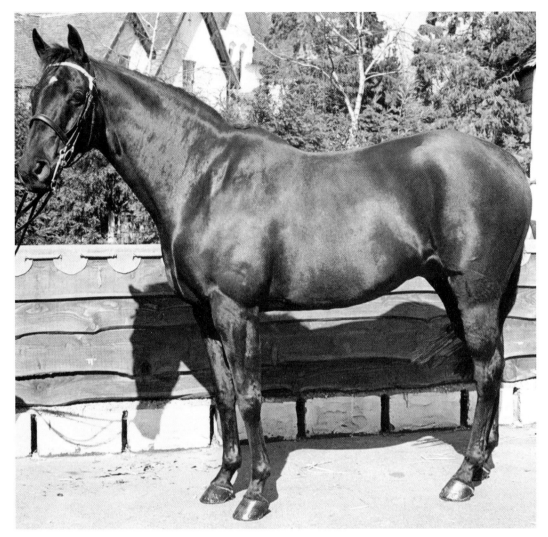

Desert Song, a Thoroughbred hack, has retired from the show ring and is competing in dressage.

lead to trouble. Make a mistake with a more 'common' horse and he will probably forgive you: a Thoroughbred might not. It will also remember when it has taken advantage of you and expect to do the same next time.

If you find and can get on with a nice Thoroughbred, you will have a very good horse. And whatever kind of show horse you buy (with the exception of the cob) you can guarantee that there will be a percentage of Thoroughbred blood there somewhere. Obviously the higher the percentage, the more Thoroughbred characteristics a horse is likely to show: a three-quarter-bred will probably be sharper than a half-bred. Having said that, there are exceptions to every rule and it is amazing how just a dash of 'common' blood can impart a lot of common sense.

Cleveland Bay

The Cleveland Bay was originally a coach horse, and when roads were improved and he became too slow he was crossed with the Thoroughbred to produce what was then called the Yorkshire Coach Horse. The Cleveland/Thoroughbred is still a popular cross in many disciplines, but the Yorkshire Coach Horse no longer exists as a distinct breed.

The Cleveland Bay is always, as its name suggests, bay with black points. Usually between 16hh–16.2hh, it has clean legs with plenty of bone and a powerful back end. The minus points from the riding horse point of view are a tendency to be straight in the shoulder and upright in the pastern – a legacy from its coaching ancestry.

When crossed with the Thoroughbred you get a quality horse with plenty of substance. They are often good jumpers, and frequently make their mark in working hunter classes. Some can be particularly strong-willed, and if you get one with a 'stroppy streak' you will certainly know about it.

Irish Draught

If the Arab is the most beautiful horse in the world, the Irish Draught – or to be more accurate, the Irish Draught cross Thoroughbred – is probably the most versatile. The pure-bred Irish Draught is a true workhorse, with a deep body, plenty of bone and little feather. Cross it with the Thoroughbred and you get extra quality, but usually the same lovely temperament.

Irish Draught stallions are usually big animals; it is not unusual to find them standing 17hh or over. But because of the breed's characteristic laid-back but brave temperament, they are often ridden and competed on as well as performing their stud duties. Irish Draughts are surprisingly agile for their size, and will often 'find an extra leg' when necessary – a quality which some people believe is in-bred and caused by them being hunted over banks and ditches as soon as they are broken! Their worst conformation faults are a tendency to be short in the neck and upright in the shoulder. These traits are sometimes, though by no means always, evident in first crosses. One thing is for certain: if someone has a horse for sale that is known to be Irish Draught cross Thoroughbred, he will never try and disguise its breeding. In fact, there are probably more 'Irish' horses offered for sale than Ireland could ever produce!

Warmbloods

Warmblood is, in theory, a term used to describe horses that are the results of Thoroughbreds or Arabs crossed with heavier breeds. In modern practice (inaccurate as it may be) it is now most often used to refer to Continental horses, bred either in their country of origin or in Britain.

There are many kinds of warmblood, including the Dutch, Danish and Swedish warmblood, the Trakehner, the Hanoverian, the Holstein, the Selle Francais and so on. Over the past few years they have become popular and successful in dressage and show jumping, but have yet to find universal acceptance in showing. That is changing, though; it used to be said that a warmblood could never gallop fast enough to keep itself warm, but in the past few seasons a few have proved that they can and as a result have done well in show hunter classes.

If you get a good warmblood, you get a good horse. He will also be an expensive one; the Continentals have breeding, producing and marketing down to a fine art that makes us look like amateurs, and they achieve prices for their youngstock at specialist auctions that make British breeders weep. If you have between £30,000 and £100,000 plus to spend at the Performance Sales International or Verden auctions, you could buy a possible world beater.

Unfortunately the aura and mystique of the top horses made warmbloods so fashionable and desirable that people in Britain rushed to buy anything that was imported. Not surprisingly, much of the stock that was imported was second rate, with conformation faults such as boxy feet and upright pasterns that predisposed many of them to navicular disease. Common sense now seems to prevail again, and people realise that warmbloods have to be assessed as carefully as any other animal; those magic breeding lines do not guarantee a sound horse.

There are, of course, many top class warmbloods and warmblood crosses bred in this country. One example is the success of Mrs Jennie Loriston-Clarke's Catherston Stud, home of many top class stallions.

If you can find a warmblood with the right conformation and movement, you could have a potential top class show horse. Remember that it needs to be the right sort of movement: your hunter, for instance, must really gallop.

You also need to be sure that your temperament is compatible with the warmblood's. They are generally laid-back, which can be an advantage, but it can sometimes be carried to extremes. There is an old joke that the German soldiers rode Hanoverians to war to make sure that they were good and mad when they got there!

Those who admire warmbloods say that they have wonderful temperaments. Those who are not so enthusiastic say that they are simply thick. Certainly they tend to need constant reinforcement of schooling, and some have a tendency to nap. There is one school of thought which says that this is an inbred tendency; Continental horses are usually stabled much more than our horses, and for many the daily routine consists of going from the stable to the manège and back again, with very little riding out in open country. Irish horses, on the other hand, are bred to go across open country and meet all sorts of hazards from day one. Whether this theory holds water or not is a matter of opinion, but certainly some warmbloods seem to lack the natural boldness of other breeds when coping with new sights and sounds.

Chapter 3
Conformation

A lot of people will tell you that it does not matter what a horse looks like as long as he does his job well. There are certainly a lot of good show jumpers and eventers that would not win prizes in the show ring, but there are very few with the sort of conformation that would predispose them to unsoundness – and those that do fall into this category generally do not last very long.

Conformation is important, because a horse that is put together correctly will stand up to the stresses and strains of work, whether he (or she) is a show horse or an eventer. He will be more of a natural athlete, and will be more likely to stay sound when asked to work reasonably hard. It should go without saying that no horse can cope with constant galloping and jumping on hard ground, but the horse with the right 'make and shape' will inevitably be the toughest.

Good conformation is not just a showing judge's idea of what looks pretty. It is a blueprint for efficiency: think of the horse as a machine, with lots of parts that can go wrong. If he has weak hock joints, forelegs and/or feet that cannot stand up to work or a short, thick neck that makes it impossible for him to flex without interfering with his breathing, the machine will not work properly.

You have to accept that there is no such thing as a perfect horse. All will have good and not so good points of conformation – though with a show horse, you hope that the good points far outweigh the bad ones. But if you pick a horse with the right basic framework he will find it easier to do whatever work you ask of him and you will find it easier to produce him at the peak of condition.

Your task is to try and work out whether the horse is shaped to do the job you will ask of him; the skill lies in deciding what faults are acceptable and what are not. For instance, can a weedy neck be built up with the correct work? A good horse vet will be able to tell you what the horse's faults are and whether, in his or her opinion, they make him unsuitable for your purpose – but not all horse vets are experts on showing, nor can you expect them to be.

Judging conformation, 'getting an eye for a horse', takes practice and everyone has pet likes and dislikes. Looking at photographs of horses that have reached the top of their sport can be very interesting; you will see a lot of well-made horses and a few that seem to break every rule in the book. The latter, though, would probably have been far less successful in the hands of an everyday rider.

It is important that a show horse moves well, and certainly that it moves straight. Usually good conformation means reasonable movement, but there are exceptions. Occasionally you come across a horse you would not look twice at which surprises you by moving exceptionally well, and there are also horses which look wonderful standing still but turn out to be a big disappointment when they move.

So what makes for good conformation? Basically it is a horse whose individual parts have no glaring faults and add up to a harmonious overall picture. Your first impression should be of a front end that matches a back end and a body that looks as if it belongs to its legs. The horse need not be in good condition – in fact it can be easier to judge the conformation of a poor horse, because it is easier to see his skeletal structure.

Look at the horse standing square on ground that is as level as possible. Ideally his body (without his head and neck) should fill a square. The classic proportions are said to be that the length of the head should be the same as the length of the neck, the girth should be the

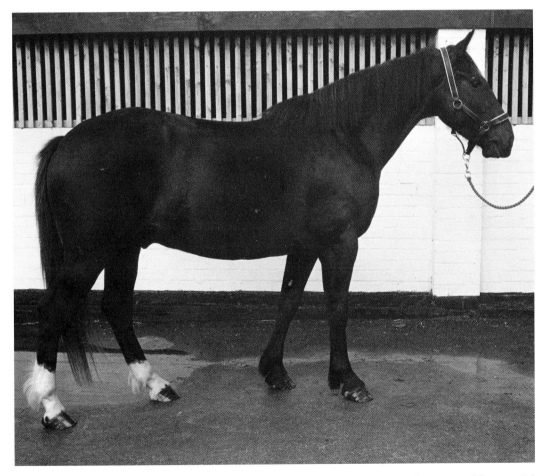

Assessing conformation means looking past the hairy heels. This is Mars, a four-year-old, potential top class lightweight cob.

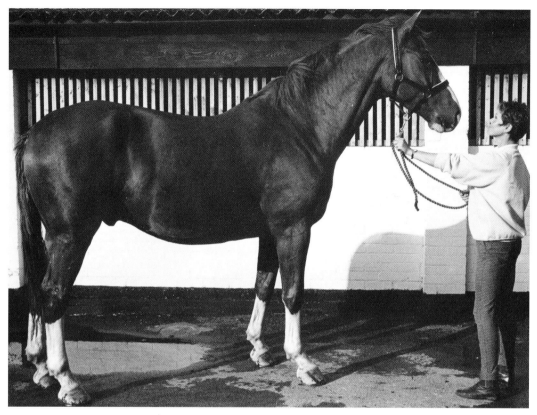

This novice heavyweight hunter, Baileys Flash Gordon, is a striking chestnut with four white socks. He has quality, substance and bone.

same 'length' as the legs and the height should be the same as the horse's length from shoulder to the end of his croup.

Head, neck and shoulder

When you look at a horse, your first impression is usually of his head. In some ways this is his least important part, because a plain head will not affect his ability, but it can give you an indication of his general character and breeding. If he puts his ears flat back when you approach him it seems optimistic to hope for a nice temperament, and for some reason a horse with a prominent bump between his eyes will often be awkward and show a tendency to nap.

It is always nice to see a big eye, but this is not essential and is not an accurate guide to a horse's character. Small eyes do not have to mean a bad temperament, though a judge may assume even without realising it that the horse is ungenuine. Showing the whites of the eyes is supposed to be a sign of wildness, but this is not always true. It can be simply that some horses have more white than others. What often does seem to be significant is the horse who wrinkles the bottom of his eyes. Approach him from various angles, and if you see bags forming in the under-eye area, make a note to be cautious!

A horse's ears can tell you a lot about its personality. Ideally they should be delicately made and pointed forwards; lop ears or ones that are generally big and floppy detract from the horse's looks and can be a sign that he lacks breeding (though you can get lop-eared Thoroughbreds). Obviously the size of the ears should be appropriate to the size of the head, but they should be small in proportion to it.

You need to look at the horse's mouth, not only to tell his age but to see if he has any problems which could affect the way he eats. The upper and lower incisors should meet evenly and he should not be badly overshot or undershot. The first is when the upper jaw is too long and is often called parrot mouth, because it has the shape of a parrot's beak. The second is when the upper jaw is too short, and again in bad cases the horse will find it difficult to eat. While you are looking at his teeth, check that the edges of the front incisors do not show excessive wear, because this can be a sign of crib biting.

The size of the head does not matter as long as it is in proportion to the rest of the horse. Your choice of tack can enhance his appearance considerably, and a workmanlike hunterweight bridle can make a plain head look quite handsome.

What is important is the way the head is set on to the neck. You need enough space behind the jawbone for the horse to flex easily; if there is not enough room his windpipe will be bent when he is asked to work in the correct position and his breathing will be restricted. A horse with this conformation fault will often make a noise; it is something cobs and animals with short, thick necks are prone to.

There are three incorrect types of neck, the ewe neck, the swan neck and the short, thick neck. Slight problems may be acceptable, but avoid any horse where they are exaggerated. However much schooling you do, the horse will never look right or be able to go in a correct way.

Sometimes people are confused about the shape of a horse's neck because the animal is thin and lacking in muscle. In this case, run your hand down the vertebrae and you will be able to see if they form the straight line required or whether you have a conformation problem.

Ewe necked horses have an 'upside down' outline and cannot flex properly. They often go with hollow backs, and can be prone to foreleg problems because their centre of gravity is shifted forwards. Short, thick necks give the rider the impression that he has nothing in front of him, and can cause flexion and breathing problems. Swan necks, with a pronounced curve, and overtopped necks with a heavy crest do not look very attractive and are unacceptable in show horses.

When you look at a horse's topline everything should flow on nicely into curves, as opposed to angles and points. The withers need to be well defined, as otherwise you will have difficulty in keeping your saddle in the right place, but preferably not too high. Cobs often have very little wither, and saddle fitting is important.

The shape of the shoulder affects the sort of ride a horse will give you. You will often hear a horse described as having a 'good front', but do not confuse this with having a 'good length of rein'. The latter means that the horse's neck is long enough, but a good front is much more important and is dictated by the slope of the shoulder.

A nice sloping shoulder, good withers and correct length of rein means you are halfway there, because the horse should be a comfortable ride and the saddle will sit properly in the middle of his back. An upright shoulder makes for a shorter stride and the horse will be far less comfortable.

Body

The ideal frame is reasonably compact, though not overly so or the horse may have a tendency to forge and overreach. If you think he could do with a little more length, look at the rest of him: a good shoulder can compensate, but an upright horse with a short back will give you problems keeping the saddle in place.

Long backs are a sign of weakness, and again the severity of the problem determines how much worry it should cause you. Mares are usually longer in the back than geldings – and a slightly long back makes it easier to fit a side-saddle, if that is where your interest lies. A roach back, with a convex outline, is unsightly but can be acceptable as long as it is not too pronounced, and the same applies to a slightly hollow back. Bear in mind that any deviation from the ideal reduces the horse's weight-carrying ability.

Whatever the length of the back, you must have a decent depth through the girth and well-sprung ribs. A shallow girth means that there is less room for the heart and lungs, which in turn means the horse will not have the stamina or mechanical efficiency of a deeper bodied one.

You should only be able to get a handspan between the last rib and the line of the thigh – perhaps a little more in a mare, whose body is of course designed to leave room for a foal. A horse with a lengthy gap here tends to leave its back end behind when moving naturally and is harder to put and keep condition on.

It is also difficult to keep a herring-gutted horse looking well and you will need a breastplate or breastgirth to stop the saddle from slipping back (both of which are unacceptable in the show ring). This sort of horse looks 'run up', like a greyhound; he will look as if he has run the most gruelling race of his life when he is just standing still.

Many people forget that the depth of a horse's body affects the amount of weight it is able to carry. Bone is a major factor, but a horse that has ten inches of bone and a good, deep body will be up to far more weight than a shallow girthed one with the same foreleg measurement.

When you are studying a horse you need to look at it from all angles: from the front, from behind and from both sides. The impression should be one of symmetry; if there is more muscular development on one side than the other it could be the sign of an old

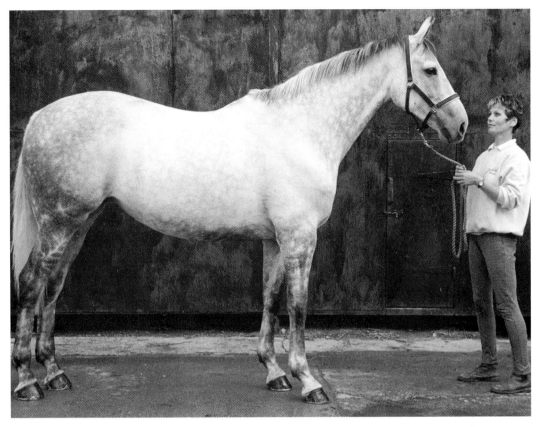

Wishful Thinking's excellent conformation means that when her ridden showing career is over, she can go on as a hunter broodmare.

injury. For instance, look at it from the back to see if there is any indication of a dropped pelvis – the muscles should be equally developed on both sides and when the horse walks away from you its quarters should not drop more to one side than the other.

When you stand in front of a horse you should see a chest that is neither too wide nor too narrow. The old grooms used to say that you ought to be able to fit a broom head between a horse's front legs.

An animal that is too narrow is sometimes described as having 'both legs coming out of the same hole'; there will not be enough heart and lung room and it will often move badly. A horse with too wide a chest will probably have a rolling sort of gait, but this is less of a fault. As with all conformation points, you need to keep in mind the type of horse you are dealing with – a nice chunky cob will look wider in the chest than a lightweight Thoroughbred, though both may be perfectly in proportion.

The last part to consider before moving on to the limbs is the hindquarters. The area behind the saddle is the horse's engine, and obviously important, but it is also the part that can be built up by correct work and feeding. Textbook conformation asks for a flattish, broad croup and well set-on tail, but a goose rump (where there is a pronounced bump at the top) is said to be a sign of jumping power, and a tendency to this might not be marked down as much in a working hunter as in his show counterpart.

A well-bred horse will have a fine, straight tail carried well from its quarters. His more common relative will have a thick, wavy one that is often set on low and tucked in. A high tail carriage where the tail goes straight out in line with the spine is often a sign that the horse has some Arab blood.

Limbs

You only have to watch a horse galloping or jumping to see how much strain is put on his legs and feet. They have to be well made to stand up to work, but perfect limbs are rare. And while it is nice to find a horse with clean (unblemished) legs a horse with a few miles on the clock may well have a few lumps and bumps; again, you have to work out what is acceptable and what might affect his soundness, performance and chances in the ring.

When you look at him from the front, you should be able to draw two lines from the points of his shoulder to the ground that are parallel, bisect the forelegs and make angles of 90 degrees with the ground. From the side, a perpendicular line should bisect the foreleg, touch the bulb of the heel and form a 90 degree angle with the ground. Deviations from these guidelines are conformation faults – not necessarily ones that will make you reject the horse, but which should be taken into consideration when you build up your overall picture of his good and bad points.

If the measurement between the centre of his hooves is greater than that between the points of his shoulder, he is base wide – something you often find with narrow-chested horses, and which can put extra strain on the inside of the forelegs and feet. If you have the opposite situation, he is base narrow and the outsides can suffer extra concussion. The forelegs should be nice and broad coming out of the shoulder and extend into a long forearm and short cannon bone. This will produce a long stride without too much knee action – in other words, a comfortable ride.

The knee is also important, because it is a working joint. It should be wide and flat; broken knees, which sound alarming but do not have to be, are unacceptable in the show ring. They usually mean that the horse has fallen and broken the skin, which has healed to leave a blemish. You need to ask yourself, though, what made him fall or trip in the first place: a one-off accident is self explanatory, but if he trips or stumbles habitually it is usually a sign that he is either weak and on his forehand or that there is a more sinister reason such as navicular disease.

There are three common faults in this area: back at the knee, over at the knee and tied at the knee. A horse that is back at the knee puts extra strain on his tendons, because he has a concave outline between the bottom of the knee and the top of the fetlock. Over at the knee is the term used to describe the opposite, where the outline is convex; in bad cases the horse can look as if he is about to fall over. Both might be acceptable as long as the problem is only very slight. A horse that is tied at the knee has a marked indentation at the back of it. It puts a slight strain on the tendons, but unless it is a marked defect you may decide that this alone is not enough reason to turn down an otherwise good horse.

The cannon bone should be short. Check for splints (bony growths on the splint or cannon bones) that are usually caused by strain or blows. They are usually situated on the inside of the leg, though you can get them on the outside, and you are more likely to see them on a foreleg than a hind. Once they are formed they do not usually cause problems unless they are in a position that interferes with the knee joint, but a judge will mark down any horse with less than clean legs. Acquired marks such as scars are usually accepted in working hunter classes, but even then they will count against a horse if the judge cannot decide between him and another.

A horse's weight-carrying ability depends to a large extent on how much bone he has. This is a measurement taken round the widest part of the cannon bone, just below the knee, with the tape measure as close as possible to the leg without being loose or tight. As a rough guide, a lightweight hunter should have about eight and a half inches of bone, a middleweight about nine inches and a heavyweight nine to nine and a half inches. You see far too many horses in the show ring who are light of bone, with legs that do not match their bodies.

The fetlocks, as with all joints, should look as if they are a pair. Avoid fetlocks with lumps on them, but do not worry too much about windgalls unless they are very pronounced. These are enlargements of fluid sacs around the pastern or fetlock joints and can be found in front or behind; a lot of people say that a horse without a windgall is a horse that has not done any work!

Pasterns should be reasonably long and sloping, but not in an exaggerated way. If they are too long, the fetlock drops too much and puts extra strain on tendons and ligaments. Upright pasterns are the worst fault: the horse will not only be an uncomfortable ride, because his pasterns will not absorb concussion properly, but he will be more susceptible to concussion problems like ringbone and navicular. Hind pasterns are slightly shorter than the front ones.

Now look at the hindlegs, where we want to see a well-defined gaskin or second thigh. The second thigh can be developed by work; a lot of people do not work their horses properly, ie from behind into the hand, so the animals' muscles are not built up in the correct way. Good feeding and proper schooling can change a horse's shape dramatically, but you must have the right framework to start with.

The hock joint is a very important one, because the hock is really the horse's motor. How often have you heard people talk of 'getting the horse's hocks underneath him' or 'jumping off his hocks'? In fact the whole hindleg is part of this power process, but the hock is a vital part of it. A good hock joint is wide, deep and not too straight – the ideal angle has been defined as 175 degrees. From behind, you should be able to drop perpendicular lines from the point of the buttocks to bisect the hocks, cannons and heels.

The worst kind of hock conformation is sickle hocks, where the leg is in front of a perpendicular line dropped from the hock to the ground. In bad cases, the horse can look as if he is about to sit down. Such animals find it hard to collect themselves and are usually bad jumpers, because they cannot lift their bodies enough. Cow hocks, where the hocks turn inwards (not surprisingly, like a cow's) tend not to be such a problem from the soundness point of view unless very pronounced.

A lot of strain is put on the hock joint, so not surprisingly it is an area where you can get problems. A bog spavin, the filling of the natural depression on the front of the hock, is a blemish and not an unsoundness as long as there are no bone changes. A bone spavin is much more serious and often cannot be seen by the naked eye – if the horse fails on a hindleg flexion test (see Chapter 4 on vetting) the vet may suspect that a bone spavin is to blame.

Capped hocks are unsightly and will go against a show horse. They are fluid-filled enlargements on the point of one or both hocks, usually caused by the horse kicking at the walls of its stable or lorry or by scraping himself on his stable floor because of insufficient bedding. If treated straightaway (by administering bute to reduce inflammation and massaging iodine ointment into the area) they can sometimes be brought back to normal. Laser treatment can also help.

Curbs are swellings on the back of the hindleg just below the hock. They can be 'true' or 'false'; you can tell which by picking up the hindleg. The false curb will disappear, but the true one will remain visible. Curbs often go hand-in-hand with sickle hocks, but they can form as the result of a blow. You would not want to buy a show horse with this problem.

Thoroughpins, swellings above the hock joint just below the Achilles tendons, are blemishes and will not make a horse lame – they are thought to be caused by repeated trauma and can occur if a horse has been kicked. They are not a danger in themselves, but make sure the hock conformation is reasonably good and the horse has plenty of good points to make up for this one.

Feet

Last but definitely not least, take a long, hard look at your potential purchase's feet. There is an old saying, 'No foot, no horse', and like many old sayings it has a lot of truth in it.

First check that you have two matching pairs – and look from behind as well as in front. Look at the coronet, from which the hoof grows down, and check that it is free from lumps and ridges. Be careful if one foot seems bigger or a different shape from its partner, but if you like the horse ask your vet's advice.

Sometimes you will see rings on the feet. These can be either grass rings or a sign that the horse has had laminitis (and may therefore be prone to it again). Grass rings can be

No foot, no horse! This foot is flat, overgrown and has sandcracks. It improved considerably with long-term attention from a leading farrier and the addition of a biotin supplement to the horse's feed.

caused by several things, including a change in diet (such as when the horse is brought up from grass and put into a stabled regime). Laminitis rings are more regular and spread more at the heels – do not be totally put off a horse that has these, but do take your vet's advice. Laminitis is often assumed to be a pony problem rather than a horse one, but many larger animals get it as well, especially after good summers when there is plenty of grass.

The angle of the foot is important. There should be a continuous slope from the pastern down the hoof wall, and the feet should be open and reasonably large in proportion to the rest of the body. Avoid narrow, boxy feet, a common failing with warmblood horses and a structure that seems to predispose some of them to navicular.

You want to see well-defined frogs and heels that are open as opposed to shallow. Flat feet can cause problems and horses with this conformation are prone to bruising. A good blacksmith can help this and many other problems with corrective shoeing, but do not be prepared to compromise too much over foot defects.

If the horse has been shod for a few weeks when you see him, look for signs of excessive wear that might indicate faults in the way he moves. If he dishes (throws out one or both forelegs) there might be more wear on one side than the other, and squared off toes in front or behind indicate that he drag his toes.

The size of the foot should reflect the size of the horse, but slightly small feet are better than noticeably big ones (unless he is a cob; cobs have plenty of bone and 'soup plates' to match!) Too large feet often lead to faulty movement. The horse may well brush (knock one leg against the other) especially if his front legs are a bit close together, and will tire more easily simply because it takes more effort to move over-large feet – imagine what it is like wearing size seven shoes when you should take a size four.

Small horses with too small feet often suffer from weak walls. In bigger horses the more usual problem stemming from this fault is brittle horn; there is a poor base of support and the animal can trip. Nail holes are the giveaway to brittle feet – see if the horn is breaking away around them. Added drawbacks are contracted heels and small frogs: all these mean that the foot cannot function properly, resulting in lameness problems.

Horses, like people, can also have flat feet. These are prone to corns and bruising and, because the frog grows too much, to thrush. The sole is moderately concaved in a well-formed foot, to give a good bearing surface.

A lot of people worry that they cannot tell the difference between bad feet and bad shoeing. Your vet will of course advise you, but generally you do not see much really bad shoeing in this country. Only registered farriers are allowed to shoe, and they have to train and pass exams first. You will often see overgrown feet, because many owners try and economise on shoeing by making the shoes last longer than they should, but British horses are usually pretty well done by. The worst shoeing is seen on Irish horses that have just come over, because the farmers often do the job themselves.

The more you learn about conformation, the more you realise what there is to find out. You may also be like the person who read a medical dictionary and ended up as a hypochondriac. Remember that you should have an imaginary picture of the ideal – but accept that you will never find it!

Chapter 4
Where to Buy

By now you should have decided whether you are going to show the horse you already own in the most appropriate classes, or buy a show horse on which to compete in a specific area. If you opt to buy, you have an interesting/exciting/frustrating/nail-biting time ahead (delete where appropriate) because you will probably find yourself in situations that encompass all the above, and more besides.

Buying horses is a minefield at the best of times, and no matter how knowledgeable you are, you need a bit of luck to go with it. Horses are not machines, and you cannot guarantee that a horse which goes beautifully for one person will do the same for another. The skill of the rider is a vital ingredient; you can buy the most successful show horse in Britain, if you have enough money, but you cannot guarantee that it will continue to stand top of the line unless it is ridden and produced to the same high standard.

Most people cannot afford to buy made horses, and have to buy the raw material and do the job themselves. There is a lot of satisfaction to be had; winning a rosette on a horse that you spotted as a skinny, hairy, ignorant four-year-old makes all the hassles worthwhile. Finding your show horse might not be easy, but there are ways of reducing the risks to an acceptable level.

Basically, there are three ways of buying a horse – from a private seller, from a dealer or from an auction. In between are the other avenues, buying through an agency or from a professional agent (there is a difference between the two). Years ago, anyone buying a horse was told to remember the Latin warning *Caveat emptor* – let the buyer beware – and this still holds good. At one time, you kept your wits about you and if you bought a bad 'un, you got rid of it as quickly as possible and, if necessary, put the money you lost down to experience. Nowadays litigation is the name of the game, and it can be very expensive.

Obviously you have certain legal rights whoever you buy from, but the most valuable protection for any consumer – whether you are talking about buying horses or washing machines – is the Sale of Goods Act. Sections of this state that goods have to be of merchantable quality and fit for the purpose for which they are sold: in other words, if you buy a horse that is said to be quiet to ride and it tries to throw you under a bus or bolts down the road at the first opportunity, you have a comeback.

The most valuable sections of this Act from the buyer's point of view are the ones relating to merchantable quality, and they only apply if you buy a horse from a dealer. They do not apply if you buy a horse from a private person or at an auction. If you buy a horse through an agent (someone who takes horses to sell on behalf of clients) and things go wrong, your argument can be with both the agent and the horse's owner.

The very thought of things going wrong may be enough to put you off buying horses and encourage an interest in showing budgies instead. Take a deep breath and steady your nerves, because it does not have to be that bad. All you have to remember is that it can be . . . and do all you can to ensure that it does not happen to you.

Buying privately

At first glance it might seem that the easiest way to buy is from a private seller. A look through the advertisement pages of *Horse and Hound* and other magazines will show that there are plenty of fabulous-sounding animals about, and if you are a genuine buyer it would seem reasonable to hope that you could match up with a genuine seller. Sometimes that is exactly what happens . . . but sometimes it doesn't.

The first, and biggest, drawback is that you have no protection under the Sale of Goods Act. Because of this, you should get what is known as an 'expressed warranty': a written warranty on all important points such as age, experience, height, lack or presence of stable vices, and so on. This means that if you do end up with problems, or there has been a misunderstanding over something, you have a formal back-up.

The second snag is that a lot of private sellers are unfortunately not that knowledgeable. They guess at their horse's height (usually adding on inches) breeding, type and potential and often overestimate its conformation, ability and value. That might sound harsh – and there are, of course, plenty of genuine and knowledgeable private sellers – but anyone who has ever bought a horse will tell you that it is true.

One of the biggest headaches for private sellers is knowing what value to put on their horse. You may be lucky and find someone who does not realise that their Riding Club all-rounder is a potential top class lightweight hunter, but that sort of luck is rare. What usually happens is that someone sees a horse advertised for £X,000, thinks that his horse could do what that one is supposed to and is therefore worth the same amount.

Horses can appreciate and depreciate in value remarkably quickly. A nice looking, unspoilt horse worth £4,000 can be worth much less after a few months of bad riding and incorrect schooling. There is nothing to say that it cannot be re-schooled and got to the standard its early potential promised, but there is no guarantee: and it takes skill to re-school a horse. It is a lot harder for him to unlearn bad habits than to acquire good ones.

The best kind of private sale is the one that never reaches the advertisement pages. It is when someone who knows that you are looking for a youngster to make a riding horse or small hunter also knows someone who has bred a lovely sort and is looking for the right person to bring it on, or when a horse that has done well in local dressage is looking for a new home and would also make a riding horse. It pays to have a wide network of contacts.

Buying from a dealer

The old image of a dealer was of a shady character who only sold problem horses, and knew all sorts of ways to disguise the problems. The modern version is very different; a dealer is a business man or woman out to make a living, and the only way to do that is to trade honestly. There are undoubtedly bad dealers as well as good ones, but the bad ones do not last long. If you buy a wonderful show horse from Joe Bloggs you will sing his praises to your friends, thus enhancing his reputation and attracting more customers for him. If he sells you an old screw, you will tell everyone what a crook he is and no one will want to buy from him.

Some problem horses do find their way to dealers' yards and are eventually sold on, but that is because dealers have the experience to sort out problems caused by other people's bad riding or incorrect handling. They also know that a problem for one person might be acceptable to another; for instance, some people would not accept a stable vice whereas others will put up with it for the right price. A lot of people will tell you never to buy a show horse from a dealer who specialises in them – their reasoning is that if it was any good the dealer would keep it, but this is actually a twisted logic.

It goes without saying that no show producer, be he a private person or a dealer, will sell a horse that he thinks will go right to the top. Having said that, it also goes without saying that everything has its price, and if the numbers got high enough the horse might find itself a new owner! But professionals are always looking for the ultimate: they want a cob to win Wembley, not an amateur owner/rider's class. Because they know what makes a show horse, and what the judges look for, they will often have horses for sale that will do extremely well in amateur hands. Do not forget, either, that no one is infallible. Everyone has sold a horse and regretted it sometimes, and there is always the chance that a potential superstar might slip through the net.

If you find a good dealer (and the best way is through word of mouth) and know what you are looking for, he will probably be able to find it for you if your price range is accurate enough. You will rarely get a bargain from a dealer, but you should get what you wanted at a fair price. A dealer's job is to match the right horse with the right rider, and after talking to you and seeing you ride he ought to be able to do this. But if you buy a horse and find that for some reason you do not get on with it, most good dealers will exchange or part exchange it or sell it on your behalf and take a commission.

Buying through an agent

Selling horses is just as difficult as buying them; apart from the time it involves, it takes skill to present a horse to its best advantage. Some people also find it nerve-racking or even upsetting, especially if the horse is one of which they have become fond. And, of course, there are the dreaded time wasters – the people who do not know what they want, or are simply 'seeing what's about' and actually have no intention of buying.

For these reasons, some sellers prefer to let a professional do the job for them in exchange for a percentage of the sale price and sometimes livery charges as well. A professional agent, who is usually also a dealer, can make sure that the horse is looking and going as well as possible. He or she will have the experience to work out quickly what strengths and weaknesses the horse has, what sort of home it would be best suited to and what a fair market price would be.

From the buyer's point of view, the advantages are much the same as those which apply to buying from a dealer. A good agent will know when a horse has good conformation, even if he is not a showing expert; it may be up to you to decide what category the horse fits in to, but while you may have a few disappointments over height and type, you might end up with a nice surprise!

Buying through an agency

Agencies are a relatively new phenomenon. They range from computerised operations who send out impressive looking printouts to someone who keeps a scribbled list of horses for sale and potential purchasers by the phone and attempts to match up the two. They usually charge a fee to sellers and are free to buyers: any agency which tries to charge potential buyers should be viewed with suspicion.

One problem with agencies is that however fair they try to be, they usually have to rely on descriptions supplied by the horses' owners, so you can get the same problems as with private sellers. A few actually inspect all horses before registering, and providing the person doing the inspecting knows what to look for, they should be able to provide an accurate description.

Any negotiation will be with the seller, as the agency merely provides an introduction.If you buy a horse through an agency and end up with a problem, you have no protection under the Sale of Goods Act. Your argument is with the vendor, not with the agency.

Buying through an auction

Auctions can be exciting, depressing and educational, but they are not a place for novice buyers. Again, there is no protection under the Sale of Goods Act and you usually have less opportunity to study and try a horse than with any other method of buying. The big drawback is that it is quite unusual to be able to ride a horse before deciding whether or not to bid for it, so you will have to try and decide how it is likely to feel by watching it move and perhaps being ridden by the seller.

There are nice horses to be bought, but there are also ones that no one with any common sense would want to own – so if you decide to go down this avenue, be aware of the risks and do all you can to minimise them. And no matter how careful or knowledgeable you are, be prepared to accept that you might get landed with a horse that is unsuitable. Do not make the mistake of reading that Ms Professional Show Producer bought this year's star hack from Ascot Bloodstock Sales for 1,000 guineas, and assume that you can do the same. Ms Professional will have put a lot of time, experience and skill into building up and re-schooling what may have been an unruly three-year-old straight off the racetrack.

If you fancy your chances, the first thing to do is try and get a sales catalogue in advance and read the auctioneers' terms and conditions of sale – very, very carefully. These will tell you how the sale is run, what commission is payable by the vendor and what methods of payment are acceptable. In most cases you will have to pay by cash or banker's draft unless you have made previous arrangements through the auctioneers.

When you read the sales catalogue, you will find certain phrases that crop up time and time again. It is important to understand these, because they have definite meanings – and for most people, they will be as relevant to a show horse as to any other kind. For instance, a horse that is described as a 'hack' is not one that will necessarily make a show hack, but it means that the horse must be quiet to ride and sound in action.

Easy enough, you might think . . . but it is not as clear cut as it seems. 'Quiet to ride' only means that the horse is capable of being ridden; it does not mean that the horse is necessarily safe in traffic, and there is also the consideration that one person's definition of a quiet ride might not necessarily be another's.

A 'good hunter' is a warranty that the horse is sound in wind, eye, heart and action, is quiet to ride and capable of being hunted. It does not mean that it will win rosettes in a show hunter class or jump round a workers' class. You also take the risk that the horse might be too strong for you. Best of all, 'a good mover' does not mean that the horse is bound to catch the judge's eye – it simply means that the horse is not lame.

The catalogue will also tell you whether the horse has a stable vice. Animals that crib bite, weave or windsuck must be declared as such, as must those that have been operated on for wind problems or de-nerved. Any horse that has been operated on for wind defects cannot be registered with the British Show Hack, Cob and Riding Horse Association or the National Light Horse Breeding Society and your showing would therefore be restricted to local level. If the animal makes a noise, of course, you will not do any good even at the smallest show.

There are many good reasons why people sell horses through auctions. It might be that they can get a better price, because the sale is for a specific sort of horse (such as hunters) and will be attended by many would-be buyers. It also offers the bonus that everything can be over and done with in one day, and sellers do not have to mess about with time wasters.

But always remember that an auction can be a good place to get rid of a horse with a problem. Read the catalogue descriptions carefully, and when you get to the auction (which should be as early as possible) talk to the person selling the horse. A genuine seller will be forthcoming, if only because he wants the best price. Watch out for statements like 'It's not my horse, I've just brought it for a friend'. You also need to be aware of late arrivals, horses that get there just before they are due to go in the ring. There is usually a reason why their owners do not want them to be subject to too much close scrutiny!

The terms and conditions of the sale might state that the horse is sold subject to vet, subject to the veterinary panel or subject to re-examination. This means that the auctioneers arrange for a vet or panel of vets to be present at the sale, and when you have made a successful bid on a horse you have a limited time for it to be examined.

The examination is not as full as the current five-stage pre-purchase examination, as it does not include flexion tests* – though you may be able to have a blood test taken and held for analysis if necessary. It usually costs about £30 (so is cheap at the price) and you pay this fee whether or not the horse passes. If it does pass, you pay up and take your purchase home, but if it fails, you are not obliged to buy the horse.

Buying horses is much more complicated than it used to be, and is likely to become even more so. Sadly, no one seems to benefit from increased litigation, except perhaps solicitors; you cannot get away from the fact that horses are living beings, not machines, and as such it is very difficult to apply rigid rules to their purchase. To a certain extent, you still pays your money and takes your chance, but when the lawyers become involved it gets even more expensive!

---

* Flexion tests are when the vet flexes the horse's leg joints for a short time and then makes it trot out straightaway to see if there is any sign of lameness.

Chapter 5
What to Look For

Once you have decided where you are going to look for your show horse, the search can begin. You have to be prepared for the fact that it is going to take time, money and patience, especially if you feel that it is worth travelling long distances. Some people will happily go from one end of the country to the other in search of that elusive cob, while others feel it is more sensible to restrict themselves to, say, a 50-mile radius. If you are facing long journeys, it makes sense to line up more than one horse to look at.

You never know quite what you are going to see until you get there, but asking the right questions will reduce the likelihood of a wild goose chase. Ten minutes spent on the telephone is a lot cheaper than a wasted 100-mile round trip. Double check all the basics – height, age, colour, sex – because misprints and misunderstandings are all too common.

If the horse is such a long way away you have to think twice about the time and cost of going to see it, you can always ask the seller to lend you photos or a video (preferably the latter) to give you an impression. Photos taken by amateurs can be misleading, but are better than going in blind – and a video, which should show you the horse from different angles and on the move, can be very useful. You must, of course, return any photographs or tapes whether or not you are interested in the horse.

Try and work out whether the person selling the horse is telling you facts or relying on guesswork. Has the horse actually been measured on level ground with a measuring stick, or is it an estimate? When he says it's got 'a good nine inches of bone,' is he relying on a tape measure or optimism? Has the horse's age been verified by a vet who has looked at its teeth, or through registration papers, or both? If the animal's breeding is stressed, are there papers to back it up or is it a horse that is Irish because a lot of people like them?

Ask if the horse has any blemishes, and if so where they are. It is always a bonus to find a horse with a well-made set of clean limbs, but if you are buying an older horse you are likely to find that he has the odd lump or bump. Small blemishes may not be a problem, depending on what you want to do and how good the animal is in other respects: for instance, a small scar should be overlooked on a working hunter, but a large splint will definitely go against you in a straight showing class. Usually it is a case of seeing the horse and making your mind up, but forewarned is forearmed. Unfortunately there is always the odd occasion when a not very knowledgeable seller assures you that the horse is blemish free, and you get there to find it has the worst capped hocks you've ever seen and the owner does not know what they are.

Even if you can put up with vices such as crib biting, they will affect a horse's resale value.

If a horse has a stable vice, this should be stated in the advert. If no mention is made, ask categorically whether the horse has ever been seen to weave, crib bite, windsuck or box walk. Anything other than a straight 'no' means it could well have a problem. If you get an answer such as 'He might weave in a strange box for a few days but then he'll stop' you have absolutely no comeback if you get the horse home and it weaves like a top, round the clock. Cover yourself – get a written warranty.

Whether or not you are prepared to accept a vice is a personal decision. If the horse is an absolutely perfect specimen and you can cope with it, you might be prepared to put up with it. This is especially true if you will be keeping him at home, as you might be able to find ways of controlling his anti-social behaviour – for instance, even bad weavers rarely do it in stalls, and a box walker may stop wearing out the floor if he has a sheep or goat living in his stable with him.

But think about it very carefully before taking a gamble. If the horse turns out to be not quite what you want, he will be harder to sell on than a horse without a vice. The only exceptions are horses that are particularly talented in other fields; if a show jumper sees a horse with a breathtaking jump, he will not care what the animal does in its spare time.

The biggest drawback about vices is that they are often the sign of a quirky temperament and can lead to problems in keeping the horse sound and in good condition. Weaving and box walking put a strain on the horse's limbs, crib biting and wind sucking can lead to colic, and all four can lead to the horse becoming a poor doer. Because they are nervous habits (the latest research shows that they stimulate the production of chemicals called endorphins, so the horse that weaves away in his box is actually creating his own personal 'high') they could be an indication that the horse might be difficult under the stress of competition. Vices will also affect the horse's resale value, and while you may not intend to sell him later on, you can never be sure that circumstances will not change.

While you are first and foremost buying a show horse, you are also buying a horse that you have to live with. Unless you are sending him to a professional yard to be shown and produced for you, you will be well advised to steer clear of anything that is difficult to catch, shoe or box. Professional show producers will not thank you for sending them an animal with any of these problems, but should in theory have the time and the expertise to sort them out.

Clipping is not usually an insurmountable problem; you might have to get the horse sedated until hopefully he learns that it is not as frightening or uncomfortable as he thought, but if you rug up early you should be able to get through to the end of the season before the situation arises. The worst problem in this area is the cob that is difficult to clip: they have to be trimmed and clipped regularly to look their best, and an awkward customer can be more hassle than you might be prepared to accept.

One problem that you should never, ever accept is a horse that is unreliable in traffic. No matter where you live, you are going to meet it some time – including on a showground. All the time you are asking questions, you will be building up a picture of the horse. If it becomes obvious during the conversation that this is not the one for you, say so. But if it sounds promising, make arrangements to go and look. At the risk of sounding obvious, get detailed directions where the stables are, including the exact address and (if appropriate) the 'phone number for the yard in case you get lost. It is both polite and a good idea to give your 'phone number to the seller, because if there is an emergency or if a previous visitor agrees to buy the horse, he can let you know and save you a wasted journey.

Some people will tell you that you should always arrive half an hour earlier than you arranged so that you can take the seller by surprise. This is a total waste of time, as well as being inconsiderate; if the horse has three legs instead of four you will find out just as easily at the appropriate time. Try not to be too influenced by your surroundings – you can find a nice horse at a tatty yard just as easily as a not so nice one at an immaculate place with hanging flower baskets outside every door.

First impressions

Ideally you should be taken to see the horse in his usual stable or field. If he is tied up on the yard, there may be a perfectly valid reason, but it is still a good idea to see him on his own territory at some time. First impressions can be accurate or misleading, so unless the horse is obviously very different from the description you were given, do not be too quick to write him off. Does he look reasonably happy to see you, or is he nervous or unfriendly? Never be worried if he is standing in his box looking rather dopey; some horses 'switch off' in their stables and it can simply be a sign of an easy-going type.

Notice how he is standing. Lots of horses rest a hindleg, but if he is obviously pointing a foot, especially in front, it could be a sign that something is wrong. When you open the door and walk in, does he seem interested, even if only mildly so? Do his ears flick forwards – or does he put them back and threaten you? Even worse, does he turn his back end to you and hint that if you come any closer, he will kick you?

You should be able to approach him quietly without any signs of fear or bad temper. Put a hand on his girth area and make him move over, and see that he can turn. If he tries to barge you out of the way, you know that he lacks manners and is either young and uneducated or has learned that he can impose his will on people.

Trotting up

If all seems well so far, ask to see him brought out of the stable and trotted up immediately. A lot of people will inspect a horse's conformation first, but it is a good idea to see him moving from a 'cold start' to see if he is stiff or even unlevel. This supposes that he has not been ridden that day; if someone has been to try him earlier, bear it in mind.

You have to assess two things – whether or not he is sound and whether the quality of his movement is good enough for a show horse. Ask to see him led out on a slack rope or rein so that his movement is as natural as possible. Start by standing behind and watching him walk away from and then back towards you.

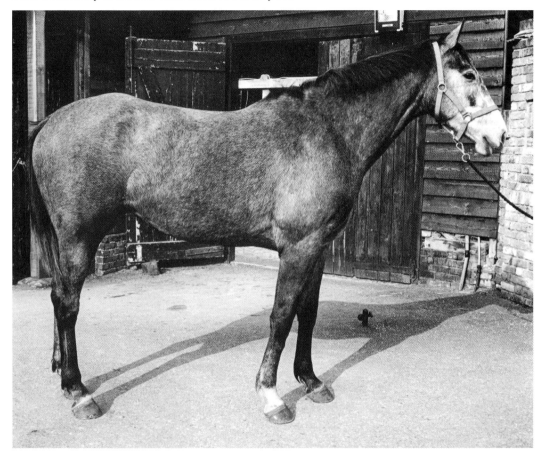

This four-year-old seven-eighths Thoroughbred, who has excellent conformation and movement, was intended to become a large riding horse. A cut to her off-fore cannon bone left her blemished and she was re-routed to a dressage career.

Ideally you should see a nice free walk with a generous stride; racehorse trainers judge yearlings on the way they walk because a horse that can walk well will also gallop. Ideally the imprints of the hindfeet will overtrack those of the forefeet by four to eight inches. You will be very lucky if you find a cob that has as good a walk as a hunter or riding horse: the walk is often their worst pace, and can tend to be short striding. There are ways of improving it, such as working them on a treadmill, but a naturally good walk in a cob is a real bonus.

Now ask to see the horse trot, again on a slack rein and preferably four times so that you can watch from the front, back and both sides. This is the pace which will show up any unsoundness and any irregularities in movement – whether the horse dishes, brushes or plaits. Dishing means that the horse throws out one or both forelegs from the knee. Brushing occurs when one foreleg brushes against the other, and can occur in front or behind. Plaiting means that the horse crosses one foot over the other, usually in front. If an otherwise lovely horse turns a toe slightly or moves a bit close behind, you might get away with it except at the higher levels, but the judge will be looking for an animal that moves straight and with a natural rhythm.

Again, there are subtle differences according to the type of horse. A hack should be an elegant 'daisy cutter,' pointing his toe but not showing any knee action. A cob or hunter will be more workmanlike, and will not show the same extravagance – many people believe that extravagant movers are not good jumpers, and even though a show hunter is not required to jump in the ring he should still be the sort of horse that the judge would want to take hunting. A riding horse should tend more towards the hunter's movement than the hack's.

On the yard

All the while you have been studying the horse in the stable and watching him move, you will have been forming an impression of his make and shape. Now you can make a firm assessment: ask to see him stand on level ground, stand back about two yards and start at the front with our blueprint for correct conformation fixed firmly in your mind!

Does he have enough chest room, or do both his legs come out of the same hole? His knees should be the same height and look as if they are a pair; white hairs or scars are a sign of broken knees and could signify either a one-off accident or a horse that makes a habit of falling over. His feet should also be a pair, and when you move to the side you should check whether he is standing level or favouring a foot.

Again from the side, you should watch the horse's breathing. There should be single inspiration and expiration: 'double breathing' is a sign of wind problems. His hocks should be nearly perpendicular, with no signs of curbs, and when you move round to stand behind him his hips should be level and equal, not dropping to one side.

Go back to the side and feel his legs. Run your hands down his cannon bones and see if you can feel any splints, bony lumps that rarely cause any soundness problems unless they interfere with the action of the knee. (You can get splints on the hindlegs, but they are not as common. Neither will win you any marks in the ring.)

Feel round the fetlocks and coronets for signs of ringbone, a bony formation that is classed as high or low. High ringbone is easier to feel and is usually the result of concussion. Either form is a good reason not to buy any horse, let alone a show animal.

The back of the heel should be soft enough for you to press it in with your fingers. If it is hard, with no give, the horse probably has sidebone (ossification of the foot cartilages). Horses usually go lame when these are forming, but then often come sound.

Some conditions, such as navicular disease, can only be formally identified with nerve blocks and X-rays, though the horse will be lame except, perhaps, in the very early stages. Horses with boxy feet and upright pasterns (very undesirable conformation) will often be prone to it, as these make them vulnerable to concussion. It often shows first when the horse is worked on a circle. A vet will do flexion tests to try and spot danger signs.

The hock is the biggest and most powerful joint, and can house all sorts of problems. A horse which moves well does so not from the front but from behind: his engine is in his hindlegs and sends him powering forwards. You never want to see a horse drag his hocks or 'leave them behind' – they should be placed well underneath him.

Spavins are common in horses with weak hock conformation. A bog spavin is unsightly and will catch a judge's eye for totally the wrong reason, but a bone spavin is much more worrying from the soundness aspect. If you pick up the hindleg, flex the hock joint for thirty seconds and then ask the horse to trot on straight away, he may go lame if a bone spavin is present. Your vet will carry out this test as part of his pre-purchase examination.

Stringhalt is another problem to watch out for. This is a nervous condition that affects the abductor muscle and causes one hindleg to be lifted higher than the other. It gets worse as the horse gets older, and there is no cure. You may only see it for a few strides in the early stages, and if you suspect it you should ask to see the horse backed up in hand and then trotted off. It should show up more clearly when he moves off, and some horses with stringhalt cannot back up at all.

Chapter 6
The Purchase

By now you will have a definite feeling as to whether or not this particular horse could be a possibility. If you have come this far and still like what you see, ask to see the horse tacked up and ridden. You may have a doubt or two but still be interested – in this case, carry on. But if at any time during the procedure you think that this is definitely not the horse for you, say so and avoid wasting everyone's time. A polite 'Thanks very much, but he's not quite what I'm looking for' should not offend anyone.

Ask a few questions while the horse is being tacked up. Is the bit the one that he is normally ridden in? (and does it match up with the information you were given at your first inquiries?) The actual type of bit is not that important; many people believe that a horse must go in a snaffle, but this is not always the kindest or most suitable bit. For showing, you will be more likely to use some kind of pelham or a double bridle – and many horses are far happier with pelhams than snaffles. You should also notice whether or not the tack fits properly; it is amazing how many people use bits that are the wrong size (usually too big) and fitted incorrectly (usually too low). Similarly, ill-fitting saddles can cause discomfort and back problems.

Observe the horse's general attitude. Does he stay relaxed and co-operative, or does he clamp his jaw and throw his head up to evade the bridle? Many horses chomp the bit when first bridled, but any mouth evasions when he is ridden, such as trying to put his tongue over the bit (or succeeding!) can cause problems. A three or four-year-old who is cutting teeth may show mouth resistances because of discomfort.

A well-mannered horse will stand still when mounted and not need someone to hold him or stand by his head. He might be cold-backed and dip away from the rider's weight at first, but you should be warned about this.

If the vendor has good facilities he might first take the horse into an indoor or outdoor school. Watch what he does with the horse: you want the chance to see all his paces. If the rider goes into trot straightaway it might be because the horse has a poor walk (which you should have spotted when you saw him led up). Similarly, if he goes straight from walk to canter it could be an attempt to minimise a bad quality trot.

It is a good idea to see the horse galloped, not to see how fast he can go but to spot any wind defects. A broken-winded horse will show the characteristic double heave of the flanks when standing, mentioned earlier. Seeing him galloped also gives you an idea of how good his brakes are – it is better to watch someone else being tanked off with than to experience it yourself.

Listen to the horse's breathing when he gallops and when he pulls up. Is he a high blower, due to excessive flapping of the false nostril, or a roarer (much more serious and caused by an affliction of the larynx)? The other noise to listen for is whistling, a higher note than roaring. It is due to paralysis of the left side of the larynx and is usually caused by a virus or strangles. Generally speaking, a noise on expiration is nothing to worry about, but a noise on inspiration is.

Nasal discharge is an associated sign that something is wrong, but is not usually permanent. For instance, a watery discharge can be an indicator of equine flu and thick mucus plus a high temperature points to the herpes virus. The latter affects the respiratory tract and is more dangerous in mares, because it can cause them to abort.

It is a good idea to see a horse ridden in the open as well as in an enclosed area. Seeing him in the school should give you an idea of how well schooled or green he is – whether he strikes off on the correct canter lead and is generally well balanced, supple and obedient (though obviously the rider needs to be capable of pressing the right buttons). If he performs as well or nearly as well in an open field he has learned his lessons well; some horses become distracted in the open and ride much greener when they do not have the support of the school walls or fence.

If you plan to do working hunters, or to take part in other activities as well as showing, you need to see him jump. A horse will inevitably jump better for someone who knows him, and who he is used to, than he will for a stranger. This is the owner's chance to show you what he can do, and if he puts him over some big fences you should not necessarily do the same yourself or worry that you might be expected to.

Finally, double check that the horse is traffic proof and is happy to leave the yard on his own before preparing to ride him yourself.

Riding the horse

Now is your chance to confirm the impressions you have built up about the horse. If it makes you feel more confident, get someone to stand by his head while you mount – you have already seen whether or not he stands still and do not need it proving again. Check that the girth is tight enough, that the stirrups are at the right length for you, and that you are comfortable before you move off. Be fair to the horse and his owner: fasten your jacket to stop it flapping around, and carry a short stick rather than a long schooling whip unless you have a particular reason for doing so and can guarantee that you will not inadvertently flick the horse with it.

Walk on, get the feel of the horse and then go into trot. Do you feel comfortable on the horse? Are you happy and comfortable? Do you feel that you want to carry on riding him? You will soon build an impression by doing a few quiet transitions and circles on either rein; if you do not like the feel of the horse (and it may be that he simply does not give the sort of ride you like) then come gently back to halt and say so. A show horse should feel comfortable, even if he is a green youngster. If he has a choppy, up and down stride (usually caused by bad conformation, which you should have spotted anyway) a judge is not going to enjoy his or her ride.

As long as you feel happy, you can carry on. Make sure the horse is happy, too – do not get hold of his head, kick him in the ribs and make him misbehave. Trying to provoke a horse into bad behaviour – to see what he will do – is unforgivable bad manners and serves no purpose at all.

Let the horse go freely forwards; when you get on a strange horse you do not say 'You will do this', but rather you ask 'Please will you do this?' How much you ask obviously depends on the horse's age and experience – an older, well-schooled horse may well come on to the bit and perhaps show some lateral work, but the owner should have demonstrated this to you. Few riders can get on a strange horse and get the best out of him straightaway, and it is important to remember that a horse needs to get used to you as much as you need to get used to him.

If all goes well you will be able to walk, trot and canter the horse quite happily and get reasonable transitions from one pace to another and back again. Then by all means ask to try him over a cross-pole; approach it in a rhythmic trot, without pushing the horse out of balance, and let him sort out his own stride. Listen to the person who is showing him to you, because he knows the horse, and be prepared to take advice.

Providing you feel confident, you can ask to canter into a small upright fence: for the average horse and rider this should be no more than two foot nine inches high. Approach it in a balanced, rhythmic canter and try and let the fence come to you; the horse should be able to sort himself out over this height. Is he as willing to jump going away from home as he is towards it?

The final test, as long as you are still happy with the horse, is to ride him on the roads. You should normally be accompanied by another rider, as you are on a strange horse and probably in a strange place, but you need to make sure that the horse is happy to go alone and is not dependant on others. Nappy horses are not worth the stable room they take up.

While you are out, vary your position, both going away from home and returning. Let the other rider go in front; you must expect your horse to want to keep up, but he should not get silly and start pulling, jogging on the spot or crabbing sideways. How does he react to the other horse? You can put up with a bit of face pulling, but be careful about the horse who lunges at a companion with teeth bared. Similarly, when you go in front your companion should keep a reasonable distance behind . . . but if he is extra cautious, does it mean that your horse is likely to kick?

When you take the lead, he should be perfectly happy: no hanging back or becoming suddenly spooky. The final test comes when you get back to the yard; ask your companion to go in but ask your horse to walk past the entrance on his own. Any reluctance, or worse still an attempt to whip round and/or rear, is an indication of nappiness.

By now you should have a good idea of whether you like the horse enough to buy it, and some people may make their minds up there and then. Others prefer to make a second visit, especially if they want to bring someone more knowledgeable along. Few sellers will quibble with that, but it is only fair to make your return visit as soon as possible (and to realise that you risk losing the horse to anyone who sees him in the meantime and is prepared to make a firm commitment).

You might be tempted to ask if you can have the horse on trial for a week or a fortnight, but few sellers will agree – and with good reason. Put yourself in their position: would you let a stranger take away your valuable horse, knowing that he might not look after him or ride him as well as you do? It also means that the horse is unavailable to other potential buyers, and if the trial is unsuccessful the seller has to go to the expense of advertising him again.

Formalities

At last, you have made up your mind and decided that this is the horse you want to buy. You have every reason to feel cheerful – but do not start celebrating yet.

Make sure that as soon as you are ready to say that you would like to buy the horse (subject to a successful veterinary examination) that you are able to pay a deposit. The amount required varies from seller to seller; some ask for £50–£100 simply as a token of good faith whereas others will want ten per cent of the purchase price. The way the deposit is paid also depends on the seller's preference, as some will ask for cash and others will accept a cheque.

Why ask for a deposit at all? Quite simply, this is done to discourage people from saying they want to buy one horse, then ringing up a day or so later because they have changed their minds and found another. Every buyer has the prerogative of changing his mind, but he should be prepared to pay for it by forfeiting his deposit to compensate the seller for lost time and other potential sales and the cost of re-advertising.

You should get a written receipt for your deposit. This should carry the name and address of the person issuing it and also of the person to whom it is issued, and be worded as follows:

> Received on (date) a deposit of £X on the 16 hands bay gelding known as Teddy. (Amend as necessary.) This deposit is taken subject to a full veterinary examination, which may include X-rays and blood tests. Should this veterinary examination be unsuccessful, the deposit will be returned in full. Should the sale not be concluded for any other reason, the deposit will be forfeited.

This agreement should be signed by both buyer and seller and it is then up to you, as the buyer, to arrange for a veterinary examination. Normally this should be done within five working days of you agreeing to buy the horse, unless there is a good reason for a delay (such as you or the vendor going on holiday).

Remember that the horse belongs to the person selling it until you have actually handed over the full price in cash or your cheque has been cleared. This final transaction is made on completion of a successful veterinary examination, which should be carried out by a good horse vet. It is surprising how many people are prepared to take the chance of buying a horse without having it vetted, but unless they are dealers who are buying and selling all the time and need to keep overheads down, this is false economy.

If you are reasonably knowledgeable, you should be able to spot obvious signs of lameness. But only a vet can tell you if a horse has an eye or heart defect, or if he has a slight irregularity in his wind that may get worse. Every private buyer should have a horse vetted: it is an investment that safeguards both purchaser and vendor.

It also means that if you pay more than £2,000 for a horse, you can insure it at a realistic value, as most companies will only insure up to £2,000 without a veterinary certificate. If something goes wrong later on, you also have ammunition for stating that it is not a pre-existing condition.

A one-horse owner should never begrudge the cost of insurance premiums. Insurance against veterinary fees is vital: it means that if your horse has an accident or is ill, you can afford to give him the best possible treatment. Loss of use is a matter for the individual, and while you are unlikely to get it for showing, it is a worthwhile option if you want to take part in other activities such as dressage or show jumping.

If you are showing a horse in a category with a height limit, it will need to be measured by a vet at an official measuring pad designated by the British Show Hack, Cob and Riding Horse Association's joint measurement board. The horse has to be measured without shoes, and there is considerable technique in presenting an up-to-height animal correctly. If in doubt, ask a showing professional to help.

Life certificates are only given at seven years, so you have to decide whether or not it is worth taking the risk that a young horse will not go over-height. Buying a three or four-year-old is a particular gamble, and all part of the fun! Remember that if you buy a horse of seven or older that does not have a life height certificate, he has to be measured in twice (not in the same year) to get it.

Chapter 7
Stabling and Feeding

Rosettes are won 90 per cent at home and only 10 per cent in the show ring. The way you look after and feed your horse – in other words, your management routine – is one of the most essential parts of the winning equation. The key word here is routine, as horses are creatures of habit, but having said that, they have to fit in with our lives rather than rule them.

A show horse has to be pretty adaptable, and there may be times when he gets his breakfast at four in the morning rather than a more civilised hour because you have an eight thirty class at a county show. Nevertheless, it is surprising how a horse who is happy and secure at home adapts to the chaos of show days; as soon as he gets back to his yard he knows he can relax and look forward to his meal. You might not be as lucky, but that is another story!

Some people are so frightened that show horses (or for that matter any top competition horse) will blemish themselves that they wrap them up in cotton wool. These poor animals are usually stabled 23 hours out of 24 and never see a blade of grass. That is not the way to keep a horse happy, and unless he is he will not perform at his best. Showing puts a horse in an artificial environment, so it is up to you to ensure that he spends some time each day in a natural one.

Daily turnout is essential, even if your turnout area is so small it provides exercise for a few hours rather than grazing. You can always provide extra food, but you cannot compensate for lack of freedom. It goes without saying that any paddock or turnout area should be securely enclosed with suitable fencing. If you are renting land or keeping your horse at a DIY livery yard you sometimes have to put up with whatever you can get, but barbed wire is totally unacceptable. Sheep wire or plain strands are often used and present a lesser risk; stout hedging and/or post and rails are the ultimate, and good electric fencing can be very useful on either a permanent basis or to create smaller grazing areas.

Sharp horses can be shown almost totally off grass in the summer if necessary. Lazy ones and good doers such as cobs will need to have their grazing restricted, either by stabling them part of the time or creating a starvation patch (a small, bare paddock with some form of shelter in it as protection against flies). Laminitis does not only affect fat little ponies; the mild weather of recent years has seen an increasing number of cases in large horses, including Thoroughbreds.

Stables must be well ventilated but free from draughts. Horses can happily withstand much colder temperatures than people think, and it is always far better to add an extra rug than to shut the top door. Over the past few years research has highlighted the desirability of dust-free management, and while there is no reason to get paranoid about it, it makes sense to expose the horse to as little dust, mould and fungal spores as possible.

If your horse is happy and fit on straw and you have a regular supply of clean bales, you are very lucky. Big heavyweight horses and cobs can have a tendency to be 'thick in the wind' even when technically sound, often because they eat straw bedding. In these cases it makes sense to use dust-free bedding and to feed soaked hay or bagged forage.

Nowadays there is an incredible range of beddings, including porous rubber matting systems which can be used alone or with a minimal amount of bedding. Horses lie down on them quite happily: nothing looks nicer to our eyes than a deep bed of golden straw, but remember that horses are not nesting animals and will lie down quite happily on bare earth. Urine drains through and away, leaving only droppings to dispose of, and this cuts down on mucking out time and manure disposal. Costs vary, but to lay matting in one stable costs on average the same as a year's supply of shavings, and most companies say their products last for at least ten years.

If you prefer a conventional bedding system, vacuumed straw is now available. You can also buy vacuuming machines for private use, but these are too expensive for anything but large yards. Other alternatives include a bedding called Auboise, made from the inside of the hemp plant, and dust-free shavings. Make sure the shavings are guaranteed dust-free, and do not be tempted by offers of free or cheap shavings which are collected from timber or building yards. These are not clean enough for animal use, as all sorts of dust, dirt and even nails can be swept up with them.

Feeding

Feeding is an art, a science and the cause of more argument and confusion than probably any other aspect of horse management. Twenty years ago working horses existed seemingly quite happily on oats, bran, grass and unsoaked hay, but a lot of things have changed since then. For a start, grassland and therefore hay is treated with more chemicals and subject to more pollution from passing traffic. The workload of the modern horse is also very different; he is usually kept as a pleasure animal rather than a working one. Instead of working on the land or hacking 15 miles to a meet and then doing a day's hunting, he will do one to two hours schooling, hacking or competing a day.

In days gone by slow, steady work was the order of the day and was much more in keeping with the horse's natural way of life. Today we demand more concentrated bursts, and feed him accordingly. The trouble is that there are so many kinds of feed and so many supplements and additives that many people are thoroughly confused.

Showing has added even more controversy to the subject, because there has been a backlash against the grossly overweight animals which have wobbled round show rings for the past few years. This can only be a good thing, because a gross horse cannot work or gallop without putting strain on his heart, lungs and legs. It is particularly dangerous in growing youngstock shown in-hand, resulting in joint problems later on.

A show horse should be well-covered and well-muscled, but not fat. He should not have a gross belly, wobbling crest or shoulders with pads of fat. Nor should he be as lean and fit as a three-day event horse, who does a totally different job. If you are unsure of how much condition your horse should carry, go to a big show and look at the horses which do well in the category you are aiming for. When you start showing, ask the judges and/or more experienced and successful competitors for advice – if you pick the right time, you will usually find that people are pleased to help.

Correct feeding depends on knowing your horse and being able to assess his physical and mental well-being. If he drops weight or is lethargic – and there can be no other cause such as a virus – you need to increase the amount and/or energy level, and if he gets above himself the hard feed should be cut back. The old saying 'You are what you eat' is as true with horses as it is with people: good food, rather than hours of grooming, produces a glossy coat. It is what you put on the inside that counts, rather than what you do to the outside.

Feeding has been made simpler with ready formulated mixes or nuts. These have been scientifically balanced to give the right levels of vitamins, minerals etc; all you have to do is choose the right energy level and work out the quantities. For most show horses, medium level energy feeds with about nine per cent protein contents are the best choice. Low energy feeds, often marketed under names such as cool or pasture mixes, are more suitable for animals in light work and high energy ones for horses with a hard workload such as eventers or hunters.

Choosing which feed to buy comes down to personal choice, and will be affected by considerations such as availability, price and, of course, whether or not your horse likes it! Most commercial feeds are very palatable, but you still get the odd horse who will eat one mix but not another.

The best feed companies have their own nutritionists, who will give free advice on their products and how to feed them. Use this as a basis, but remember that your own eye and knowledge of your horse must also come into it: horses are individuals, and one may be a good doer whilst another is hard to keep weight on. Showing is a specialist game just as much as eventing or racing, and a nutritionist with a particular interest in one field may not be as knowledgeable about another.

The traditional rules of feeding are as applicable today as they were at the beginning of the century. Always buy the best quality, feed little and often, always make sure that the horse has clean, fresh water available and always feed a succulent such as grass, carrots, etc. In an ideal situation you will give four small feeds a day, but this is not always possible for the working owner. Plenty of horses do perfectly well on two feeds a day, but if you can split the total amount fed into three and persuade someone to give him a third feed in the middle of the day, he will do even better.

The best and cheapest succulent is grass, but in autumn and winter soaked sugar beet shreds or nuts are a valuable addition to the feed. Shreds are safer, because they cannot be confused with horse and pony nuts. Some people feed sugar beet all year round, others omit it in summer because of the difficulty of keeping it fresh and stopping it fermenting in the heat. The simplest way is to keep the soaking nuts in the fridge, but if this is impossible, standing your container in a larger one of cold water keeps the contents fresh for up to 18 hours. All roots are succulents, and horses enjoy sliced apples, carrots and sometimes swedes added to their food.

In days gone by, bran was found in every feed room and every horse had a weekly bran mash as a matter of course. That was a time when broad flaked bran, which actually had a little food value, could be found: the modern stuff is more like sawdust and gives you as much value for your money. By all means feed a bran mash as a laxative *if the horse needs it*, but feeding a weekly mash as a matter of course breaks the basic rule that changes in feed should be made gradually. Bran also has a faulty phosphorus/calcium balance, so if you must feed it for any reason you must also feed limestone flour.

For the show horse, or in any case where you want to encourage the growth of a glossy coat, cooked linseed is very valuable. Most horses enjoy it, and it can also be used to help tempt a fussy feeder. Add a cupful of linseed to two pints of water, bring to the boil and simmer for at least two hours. The result is a disgusting looking jelly – which is even more disgusting if it boils over on to your cooker, so be warned.

If you buy a new horse, find out what he has been fed and, if you want to make changes, introduce them gradually. Horses have very susceptible digestive systems and suddenly changing from one feed to another can cause colic. If for some reason you cannot discover what he has been getting, start off with molassed chaff, a small amount of mix and sugar beet.

If you particularly want to feed straights (straight cereals, particularly oats and barley) there is nothing to stop you doing so. Your only problem will be that unless you have every bag analysed, you will not know the food values – with commercial feeds, you will find a printed analysis attached to every bag together with a vitamin content guarantee date. Many companies now sell oat balancer feeds designed to make up deficiencies in straight cereals.

Supplements

Look in any saddler's or feed merchant and you will see enough supplements and additives to fill a warehouse. Pick up any equestrian magazine and the advertisements run to pages. The big question is: do they have a role to play, or is it a load of hype?

The most likely answer is a mixture of both. Some products are useful, but it is too easy to waste a lot of money by buying ones that are not really meant for your horse. If he is getting a balanced diet that already contains the vitamins and minerals he needs for the work you are asking him to do, there is no point in adding more. But if he is such a good doer that you are feeding less than the recommended quantity of hard feed, a broad-based mineral and vitamin supplement, fed at half the recommended quantity, will take care of any shortfall.

Another advantage of buying commercially-made feeds is that research is continuing all the time, and formulae are altered to take this into account. For instance, we now know that horses need higher levels of fat than was previously thought.

The ever-increasing interest in 'green' issues and environmentally-sound products has led to a great enthusiasm for herbal products for horses. In one way this is going full circle, because the old grooms used to grow herbs specifically for different purposes – comfrey, for instance, was grown on studs because it reputedly helped bone growth. Horses certainly pick and choose at different types of plant in pasture – let one graze on a quiet grass verge and watch how he selects and discards – but whether this is because one tastes better than another or because he instinctively knows that a plant does him good, is hard to say.

How much value can be placed on modern herbal products is hard to say, and can only be discovered by experimentation. The most common and popular 'herbal additive' is garlic, said to help horses with respiratory problems and also to act as a natural fly repellent. A traditional aid for wind problems was to cut up a net of onions and hang it in the stable, there might be something in this one.

Probably the most useful additive you can give is common table salt. This can be either in the form of a salt lick fastened to the stable wall or, if the horse is not interested in this, by adding a tablespoonful to each feed.

Electrolytes are another recent introduction to the horse world, especially in the worlds of eventing and endurance riding. But they can benefit any horse that is working consistently hard in hot weather, and that includes the show horse.

A horse regulates his body heat by sweating, and an hour's hard work can lead to him losing about 15 litres (three gallons) of sweat. If this fluid, which contains vital mineral salts called electrolytes, is not replaced, the results can be dangerous. Horses in continuous hard work will benefit from electrolytes added to water or feed during and after periods of stress. These replace what the body loses, and any electrolytes that are not needed will be expelled.

Hay

Good hay is becoming more difficult to find, and poor quality stuff is not worth the room it takes up. Always buy the best you can get, and look after your investment by storing it correctly. A covered barn is ideal, and the first row should be on pallets off the ground. Storing expensive hay out of doors, even with a tarpaulin on top, leads to a lot of wastage. Many horses are allergic to dust and fungal spores. They must either be fed soaked hay or bagged forage. Soaking makes the fungal spores swell so that they do not get into the horse's lungs, but this only works if the hay stays wet while the horse is eating it; if it dries out while it is in the net, the problem is back.

Unfortunately soaking also removes some of the nutrients, but this is a lesser evil. Soaked hay is much heavier than dry, so split it into smaller nets (you can always hang up two at a time) to avoid hurting your back. Chucking a couple of buckets of water over it or pouring a kettleful of boiling water over it and 'steaming' it in a dustbin will not actually do any good and, contrary to hopeful and popular belief, is a waste of time.

Bagged forage, marketed under various brand names, might seem expensive compared with hay, but when you weigh up the advantages the real cost is not so bad. It is easy to store and handle, does not need to be soaked and because it contains up to 90 per cent of the feed value of grass, most people can reduce hard feed.

This kind of product, sometimes called haylage, is made from grass that has been cut and then left to dry over one of two days until it has wilted to dry matter of 45 to 65 per cent. It is then baled, compressed to half size and packed in heat-sealed bags. Do not confuse it with big bale silage, which often carries the risk of botulism.

Some horses will make a net of hay last all night, but others will pig the lot in an hour no matter how much you give them. In these circumstances, the old advice of feeding hay ad lib is not really practical. An easier way is to either put the hay in one of the special small mesh nets sold for bagged forage, or to put one net inside another, thus achieving the same effect.

The old grooms used to say that hay should never be fed until it had been stored for a year, but modern thinking is that the actual age of the hay has nothing to do with it. What is important is that new hay should be introduced gradually, as with any other feed, by mixing a little of the new with the old and gradually changing the proportions. Unfortunately no one has the answer for the horse who has not read books like this, and painstakingly sorts out all the delicious new hay or bagged forage and discards the rest on his stable floor.

Chapter 8
Preparation

It is very tempting, especially when you have bought a new horse to show, to start work straightaway. Admittedly a dealing or professional yard may do just that, but they have the experience and the expertise to know how much to ask and are used to dealing with horses that are still getting used to new surroundings. The private owner usually has time to go more slowly, and this will pay dividends in the long run.

You have to get to know your horse just as much as he has to get to know you. Four or five weeks spent just establishing a routine and riding out in his new surroundings will be well spent. It also gives you a chance to introduce the horse to people such as your farrier and, if necessary, to get his teeth rasped by your vet or equine dentist.

Shoeing

A good, reliable farrier is a big asset. If you can find one, hang on to him and make sure that your horse is booked in every five or six weeks, depending on the amount of roadwork you do. You should not leave intervals of longer than six or seven weeks between visits, even if the farrier only has to rasp and refit the shoes. If you do, the feet will grow too long, affecting the balance of the foot and predisposing the horse to lameness. If you have the choice, always have your horse shod hot, where the shoe is burned on to the foot to give a closer fit. It is impossible to get the same accuracy with cold shoeing, where the farrier fits shoes ready-made to the horse's measurements and does not have the leeway for fine adjustment that hot shoeing offers.

In general, normal weight shoes are fine for show horses. Some people use lightweight aluminium ones similar to those worn by racehorses in an attempt to get as extravagant movement as possible, but this is expensive. Your farrier will recommend a suitable weight of shoe according to the type of horse; heavier horses will normally have heavier shoes than, say, hacks who are light on their feet.

Hunters were traditionally shod with handmade shoes, and if your farrier is interested in competing for prizes which some shows offer to the best shod horse, he may also be interested in making them. This is very much the icing on the cake, as most farriers have neither the time nor the inclination to make shoes. Some people use broad web shoes on big horses, but this is not recommended as the bigger surface area increases the risk of slipping.

It is always worth having studholes at least behind, and with extravagant movers in front as well. This gives you the option of using studs whenever ground conditions mean that there is a risk of slipping. This is applicable in dry weather as well as wet; it only takes a light shower to put a greasy surface on a hard showground.

You need to keep a collection of studs so that you are prepared for all conditions. Smaller, pointed ones are suitable for hard going and square ones for when conditions are wet and boggy. Always use the smallest stud you can get away with, as the grip they give has to be weighed against the fact that they are bound to unbalance the foot slightly, and never work a horse on the roads or travel him in studs. If a horse treads on himself (or on your foot) with studs in, he can do a lot of damage.

The traditional way of keeping studholes clear is to plug them with cotton wool soaked in hoof oil. This is a fiddly, time-consuming job and there are now several forms of keeper on the market. These are designed to be screwed into studholes; some work better than others, and it is best to loosen and re-tighten them each day to prevent them becoming welded to the shoe.

Correct shoeing is, of course, essential to keep any horse sound, but it is surprising how much a skilled farrier can do to safeguard or even enhance a show horse's movement or appearance. For instance, if a horse is slightly pigeon-toed you can ask your farrier to offset slightly the toeclips on the front feet; this gives the optical illusion of the horse standing straighter than it actually does.

Hopefully your show horse already has good or at least adequate movement. Your farrier will make the most of that by keeping the feet correctly balanced and, if necessary, carrying out minor remedial work. You cannot change the basic way in which a horse moves, as to try and do so would put too much strain on the limbs and set up problems that could lead to lameness and even permanent unsoundness.

However, a farrier can offset the shoes slightly to minimise the risk of the horse hurting himself (as protective boots cannot be worn in the show ring). If the horse moves a little close, the farrier can feather the inside edge – make it narrower and higher than the outside one to encourage the foot outwards from the customary line of flight.

Young and unschooled horses who are not in balance will sometimes forge (strike the back of the front shoe with the toe of the back one). Apart from making a distinctive noise that will catch a judge's ear for the wrong reason, there is a danger of the shoe being pulled off and the horse stumbling or falling. If the hind shoes are set well back and the toes squared and rounded off, this fault can be minimised. This is only a temporary measure: it is up to you to improve the horse's schooling so that he can carry himself in balance.

Over-reaching is also caused by lack of balance, and usually happens when a horse is tired, unfit or unschooled. The front feet must be kept short, and the horse can be shod with rolled toes and raised heels. The hind shoe heels can be left slightly longer and the shoes should be well set back and rounded off. Again, this should cease to be a problem when the horse is fit and in balance.

Teeth

Before you put a bit in any horse's mouth, you should check that his teeth are in good order. It is amazing how many people will complain that their horse resists the bit (or more accurately, the rider's hand) without first checking that the animal is not in discomfort or even pain. Behavioural problems such as head tossing, opening the mouth, pulling and holding the head to one side are often a sign that the horse has sharp edges to his teeth. So too are eating difficulties, such as dribbling feed or quidding (where the horse rolls the feed into balls in his mouth and drops it instead of chewing and swallowing).

Ideally, routine care should start as a yearling when sharp edges are rasped smooth and any wolf teeth taken out. Wolf teeth, which are very small and can be present in both sexes, are best removed as a matter of course. They can interfere with the action of the bit and cause considerable discomfort, and as they serve no purpose there is no point in leaving them.

If you suspect that your horse has a problem, run your fingers down the outside of his face where the bridle touches. If anything hurts, you will be able to tell because the horse will try to move away from your touch or throw his head up. Do not put your fingers in his mouth to try and feel for sharp edges, or you risk being bitten; this hurts just as much whether the horse does it on purpose or inadvertently!

Young horses who are cutting teeth are particularly prone to mouth problems, and it is important to be aware of this. A horse sheds twenty-four teeth between the ages of two and a half and five years, so it is hardly surprising if there are times when he feels sore. Using force is a mistake that will leave you with a legacy of resistance; you simply have to accept that there will be times when a young horse is not going to go as well as you would like. It often helps to use a bit which does not move about too much in the horse's mouth and which has other control points. Many young horses (and older ones too) go happily in a vulcanite pelham, which has a mild mouthpiece and also acts on the poll and curb groove.

Some people ask their vet to check their horse's teeth when he is dealing with routine vaccinations, but there is a growing move towards specialist equine dentists. This can make sense: most vets do not have time to specialise in dentistry, and it does not form a large part of their training. The other obvious point is that if your teeth hurt, you visit the dentist rather than the doctor, and it makes sense to apply the same logic to your horse.

At present horse dentistry is a grey area in Britain. The only organisation of horse dentists is the Worldwide Association of Equine Dentists, but there is as yet no body recognised officially by the Royal College of Veterinary Surgeons. Some vets work in conjunction with horse dentists, whereas others want nothing to do with them. It is a difficult situation that will hopefully be resolved before much longer.

Schooling

Once the horse is relaxed and happy, you can start work. Whatever sort of class you will be competing in, you should have the same aims in mind: a horse who goes forward from the leg into the hand and is a balanced, responsive and obedient ride. This cannot be achieved overnight, and progress will depend to a large extent on your own riding ability.

It is assumed throughout this book that the reader is a reasonably competent rider – that even if you have just bought your first horse, you are confident in the basics. But whether you are novice or experienced, you may hit problems at some time that you cannot solve by yourself. If so, get expert help – but make certain you choose the right teacher. An 'all-round' instructor is fine when you are starting out, or if you want to compete as an all-rounder. But if you are going to specialise, whether it be in showing, show jumping or dressage, you need a specialist teacher who understands what is required and has the experience to help you achieve it. After all, if you need a builder, you do not employ a plumber, no matter how expert he might be in his own field.

Horses, like people, get bored with doing the same old thing. So while it might be tempting to spend most of your time schooling in an enclosed area, make sure you vary what you do and where you do it. It is all very well having a horse that canters perfect circles in an outdoor school with no distractions, but what happens when he is asked to work in a show ring with exciting things happening all around him and other horses going in all directions? Even the newly-broken horse should be taken out and shown what life is about as soon as he understands how to stop and start and go through the gears, and you have enough control to be safe.

Variety – working in a schooling area, hacking out, working in the open field and perhaps jumping – will keep your horse interested. But whatever you are doing, he must be *working*. Hacking is not an excuse to slop along on a loose rein admiring the scenery. He must walk out in an active, rhythmic walk, go forward into trot when asked and come back equally happily.

The walk is the most difficult pace to improve and the easiest to spoil; too many people are so busy concentrating on the front end that they forget about the importance of going forwards, and the horse either takes short steps or jogs. Some horses have a naturally good walk, others do not. Cobs, because of their short legs, often find it difficult and must be ridden correctly. If you try and hustle them too much, they tend to jog.

One of the most effective ways of improving a horse's walk is to work him on a treadmill, which encourages him to stride out without being hampered by the rider's weight. These are expensive machines and not viable for the one-horse owner, but if you are lucky you may be able to find a professional yard with one to hire. Most horses adapt to them quite happily, but it is important that they are introduced to it by an experienced operator.

The walk is the pace that racehorse trainers and the old hunting grooms use to get horses fit and to harden their legs. The trot may well be the pace you use most frequently

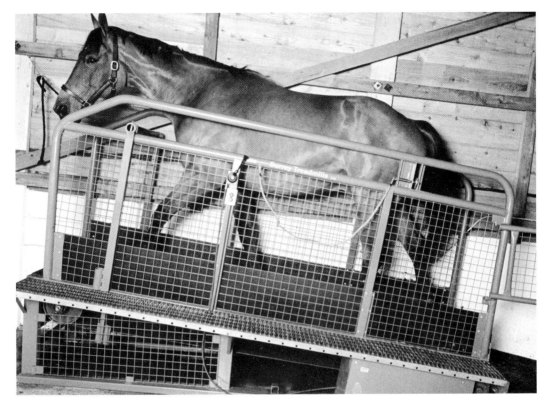

A treadmill can be an excellent aid to getting a horse fit and improving the walk.

in schooling, but trotting on the roads should be kept to a minimum to reduce concussion. Hard ground causes more problems than anything else.

Some riders introduce lateral work (which teaches the horse to go forwards and sideways at the same time) to their horses' schooling, but this must be done with care. A perfect canter half-pass may look very elegant in a hack class, but unfortunately not all judges are brilliant riders. If one gets on your horse, puts his or her leg too far back and wonders why the horse is going sideways, there is likely to be confusion all round – and especially on the part of the poor horse. If in doubt, keep your schooling simple: it is the basics that count.

Different types of horse inevitably give a different type of ride. A hunter or cob will be more workmanlike, more onward bound and able to gallop, whereas a hack will be light and elegant. Even so, the essentials remain the same.

Requirements in the ring

All show classes require the horse to be trotted up in hand, and most ask you to gallop in company. Watch any class at a local show and you will get plenty of demonstrations of how not to demonstrate these skills. Watch a class full of professionals at a large show and you will (hopefully) see how it should be done. Horses have to be taught to trot-up and gallop; do not make the common mistake of thinking they are the easy part of a class that comes naturally.

Many horses are lazy about being run-up for the judge. This can often mean the difference between winning and being farther down the line, because it gives the judge a chance to assess the horse's paces at close quarters without the rider's interference. A good rider can disguise a lot of faults in a horse's way of going, but it is harder to do this when you are both on the ground and the judge is looking at you and you alone.

Practice at home, preferably on a level area bounded on one side by a fence of some kind: this helps prevent the horse swinging his quarters away from your essential trotting up aid, a schooling whip. He should wear a bridle rather than a headcollar to give you maximum control, and should walk on briskly when asked to do so. You should neither be dragging him along nor have your arms pulled out as he barges off.

If he lags behind, tap him on the girth with the schooling whip – quite hard, if you need to – until he smartens up. If he pulls, give several sharp pulls on the reins rather than one continuous haul. Sticking your elbow in his chest can give you more leverage, but if he is bigger than you and knows it, a bit of brute strength from someone rather larger can help persuade him of the error of his ways. If you are positive enough, this is rarely necessary: you sometimes have to forget finesse to get the message through.

The horse should go forwards into trot immediately he is asked; by all means give a click, but do not say 'Terr-ot' in a loud voice as per the lungeing handbooks unless you want to amuse the judge. If he does not go straight off when asked, use the schooling whip again. Unfortunately some experienced show horses become very crafty and will try and lag behind in the actual show ring. If this happens, it is acceptable to use a helper to wave a stable rubber discreetly at the horse as you move out of line to start your trot-up. Make a mental note to do some practising when you get home, if necessary getting a helper to hide round the corner with a lunge whip; when it has been cracked behind him a few times, the horse will soon decide it is less trouble to behave.

Galloping a horse in the show ring is an art in itself. Horses have to be taught to gallop correctly under saddle, but it must be done correctly. You do not want a flat-out charge down the side of a field; the judge is looking for a smooth acceleration of pace and lengthening of stride and an equally smooth and controlled deceleration. Too many people think that sheer speed is the key, but this is not the case. The most important thing is to keep your horse in balance; come round the corner in a nice, balanced canter and open up down the long side of the ring. Think of lengthening the stride as you go past the judge rather than increasing the pace, and ask the horse to come back to you well in time for the next corner.

It may help with a lazy horse to canter him alongside another, more experienced horse to give him an idea of what is required. As the schoolmaster is asked to go on, your horse

Working hunters must perform in all sorts of going. This horse shows tremendous technique even in the wet. He wears protective boots for schooling, which are now allowed in the ring.

should naturally want to catch up. Make sure that the schoolmaster is just that and has a competent jockey – the last thing you want is for the two horses to think 'Whoopee!' and decide to stage their own race.

Once your horse has the idea, leave it at that. Horses soon learn to anticipate in the ring, when they are galloping in company. Galloping inevitably puts a strain on legs and feet, and they get enough of that at the summer shows without adding to it at home.

Hack and riding horse classes always demand an individual show, though you should not be asked to do this in hunter or cob classes unless the judge has a particular and unusual reason for doing so. The golden rule with individual shows is to keep them simple: the judge wants to see that your horse is an obedient and responsive ride, not that he can perform movements more suitable to an advanced dressage test.

Your show should include walk, trot and canter on both reins, with a simple change of leg. If your horse always performs a correct flying change, fair enough, but a correctly executed simple change – where the horse comes back to trot for two or three strides before striking off on the new canter lead – is infinitely preferable to a bungled flying change. Keep your reins in both hands throughout: judges will not be impressed by a rider who holds the reins in one hand and waves a showing cane about in the other, supposedly to demonstrate the control he or she has over the horse. You see this quite often in riding horse classes at local shows, but not at larger ones.

Riding horses should be asked to show a gallop, which is usually performed down the long side, but hacks never gallop in the ring. Keep your show short – it should last about a minute to a minute and a half – and finish with a good, square halt; obviously you want the judge to see your horse to its best advantage, but remember that he has a class to judge and a timetable to keep to. If 20 riders each perform a three-minute show, the judge will soon be both bored and cross and the class will over-run.

Individual shows should be worked out at home, but do not practise them so much that the horse either becomes bored or starts to anticipate what comes next.

Jumping

Working hunter and working cob classes can give the amateur owner/rider a lot of fun – provided the horse is well-schooled in basic jumping techniques and is introduced to the variety of fences he is likely to meet in the ring. This can range from ditches and water jumps to bullfinches, hedges with very high, thin tops that have to be jumped through rather than over.

At local level, you are unlikely to find working cob classes. There is nothing to stop you entering your cob in a working hunter class for experience, and you may even be placed – some local judges take the attitude that a cob is an excellent hunter and will overlook the difference in type. You have to accept, though, that others will think differently and will automatically put you down the line no matter how well your cob jumps.

Working hunters must jump anywhere – even in fog.

Local novice working hunter classes usually start at about two foot six with a course of six to eight jumps. These will be pretty basic rustic fences and will usually include a small brush, a one or two stride double and perhaps a gate and a stile. At county level, you are entering a different ball game altogether.

Here you will be expected to jump a course similar in height to a Newcomers show jumping class, three feet six inches to three feet nine inches. If your horse could not jump round a Newcomers, you should not be thinking of competing in a county class. The standard of jumping at this level varies considerably, and many very nice horses are let down by lack of jumping training. Talk to the experts and you will often find that they have taken their young horses show jumping indoors during the winter. The going is good, the horse gains experience and confidence and is ready to face anything a working hunter course builder is likely to build.

If you are teaching a young horse to jump from scratch, get help from a show jumping trainer unless you are very experienced. Gridwork teaches him to be athletic and you can achieve a lot with just three fences; you can build various grids to improve the horse's technique.

A horse who dangles his front legs can be taught to pick up much more cleanly by using a single pole vertical with two poles placed in a V-shape on the rail. Start with the V-poles about six feet apart, then close them in gradually until they are touching. If a horse jumps to one side or the other rather than straight, and you are not throwing him off-balance by leaning to one side, use a drop pole from one wing. This should go from right to left if the horse deviates to the right, and vice versa if he swerves to the left. A horse with a poor technique behind can be helped by a grid which includes spread fences, and bounce fences (where the horse lands and takes off again without taking a stride) make him use his brain and his athletic ability.

It is always best to have a helper on the ground when jumping, not only for safety reasons but so you do not have to keep getting on and off to move poles and alter distances. A reasonably knowledgeable assistant can also make sure that you are not doing anything to hinder the horse; when you work on your own all the time, it is too easy to fall into bad habits without noticing.

Two poles placed to form a V in the centre of the fence will encourage the horse to jump in the centre and pick up his front feet. The rider, Ken Spencer, is giving the horse complete freedom of head and neck over the fence.

Early work should be done in trot. This gives you more control, because everything happens more slowly, and the horse learns to use his back end. Never make the mistake of confusing impulsion with speed: any horse can, if ridden properly, jump two feet nine to three feet six quite happily out of trot. As your work progresses, you can alter the distances and canter into your grids, then canter into a single fence.

Many horses spook and back off their fences when first introduced to jumping in the ring. The best introduction is to find a novice class at a local show and trot round it; if the horse wants to canter on, let him, but come back to trot in the corners. Clear round jumping can be another alternative, but only if there is enough room in the ring to avoid the necessity of sharp turns. If the set clear round course is tight and the ring steward does not mind, there is nothing to stop you ignoring it and devising a more suitable, flowing one.

Working hunters and cobs need to jump in an onward bound rhythm at a hunting pace. This means the horse should take you to the fence at a fair pace, but be balanced and well in control. Forget about 'seeing a stride' – if you keep a good canter rhythm, the fences will come to you. Any successful show jumper will tell you that it is the bits between the fences that count rather than the fences themselves, and that a horse must be in balance on the flat if he is to jump well. If a horse cannot canter and make changes of direction on the flat, you cannot expect him to manage this over a course of fences! It is worth taxing your ingenuity to build some working hunter-type fences at home. Plastic bags can be weighted down under a schooling fence to imitate water, and you can either dig a tiny ditch or look for one out hacking. When you introduce a horse to ditches, make sure that the take-off and landing are secure; if his footing gives way, he will not be very keen to approach it again. Bullfinches should start as a few twigs stuck into an ordinary brush, with the number being increased as the horse gains confidence.

Some people put protective boots on their horses for schooling at home; others only use them for jumping. Plain coloured boots are now allowed in the jumping phase of working hunter classes.

Chapter 9
Tack and Clothes

Showing is all about creating the right impression, and to do that both you and your horse must be properly equipped and well turned out. Tack is one of the most vital ingredients for success, not only for the sake of appearance but to ensure that your horse is comfortable and you have seemingly effortless control. Fit is everything – tack that is the wrong size or wrongly adjusted will result in an unhappy, resistant horse. And while the right saddle and bridle can enhance and even change a horse's appearance, the wrong ones can emphasise faults in conformation, or even create the illusion of ones that do not actually exist.

First impressions are vital. When you walk into the ring, the judge takes in the horse's head, shoulder and general appearance and will already be starting to sort the horses before him into some order of preference. If a horse goes past him with a brass browband hanging down and a saddle with knee rolls that cover up its shoulder, it will not come very high up in his estimation – no matter how nice it is. But if the same horse has a bridle of the right type and weight, fitted correctly, and a saddle that sits nicely behind the shoulder, it has every advantage.

Bridles

The commonest mistake amateur producers of show horses make is to use bridles that are too lightweight. They are under the mistaken impression that a lightweight bridle gives a horse's head more quality, but it does not work that way. A bridle should always be workmanlike, even for a hack or a riding horse – you should use a lighter weight than for a hunter or cob, but do not go to the other extreme and choose a bridle that looks as if it is made out of shoelaces. You sometimes see bridles made of very narrow, rolled leather used on Arabs, but it is not advisable if only for safety reasons. If a horse spooks or shies, you are relying on leather with a low breaking strain to control it.

The weight of a bridle is defined by the width of the cheekpieces, with everything else (browband, headpiece, noseband and reins) in proportion. A hunter bridle will have cheekpieces that are three quarters of an inch wide; nosebands and browbands should be flat, and the noseband should be about two inches wide. Hack bridles should have a half inch cheekpiece and riding horse ones can either be hunter weight or slightly less; both can have either plain nosebands or ones with two layers of leather stitched top and bottom.

Top: Everything wrong! A badly fitting bridle of the wrong weight, with an incorrect brass browband and bits. The general purpose saddle hides the cob's shoulder – no wonder Cosmic looks embarrassed.

Below: Everything right. Bits are the correct type and the bridle is the right weight: note the plain, flat noseband and browband. The saddle sits just right and shows off the horse's good front.

A hack should wear a lighter weight bridle than a cob or hunter, but it should still be workmanlike. A discreet coloured browband is correct. Compare this with Cosmic's bridle (page 79).

Nosebands that are stitched to the cheekpieces are preferable to ones that are slotted, as they lie flat against the head. Only cavesson nosebands are suitable for use with double bridles or pelhams, so if a horse opens its mouth to resist the bit you need to find a way round the evasion – having first checked, of course, that your riding is not at fault and the horse's mouth is in good order. A thick cavesson, dropped down a hole and fastened tightly, often has the desired effect; failing that, you can buy a type of cavesson noseband that doubles back on itself and fastens tighter than an ordinary one.

Keep your bridle plain: you are showing the horse, not its tack. Hunters and cobs should always have plain browbands, never coloured; brass browbands are out of place anywhere except on a driving bridle. You can use coloured browbands bound with ribbon in riding horse and hack classes, but they must be chosen with care. Choose two or three colours that 'lift' the horse's head and do not have big ribbon rosettes at each end of the browband, flapping round the horse's ears. Whatever type of browband you choose, make sure it fits properly – you do not want it to either sag or pinch the ears.

You can use whatever tack the horse goes best in for working hunter classes, though the same rules of presentation apply; for instance, you should not use a coloured browband. No change of tack is allowed between the jumping and showing phases. Martingales are allowed, and there should be no change of tack between the jumping and show stages.

If your horse jumps best in a snaffle, then use one; drop, flash and Grakle nosebands are also permissible. However, a working hunter class is still a showing class, so if you have the choice always opt for a double bridle or pelham to give that 'finished' appearance.

Good quality tack is an investment, so always buy the best quality you can afford. The best show bridles are handmade and have 14 stitches per inch, but if you are working to a tight budget there is nothing wrong with machine-stitched bridles as long as the leather is good quality. The older hunter bridles have three rows of stitching rather than two, but this is hard to find today unless you have your bridle custom-made. A stitched bridle rather than one with buckles or billets makes a common head look better, but means that you cannot change bits from one bridle to another.

Plain leather reins are smart and always acceptable, though some people prefer to use laced leather for the bridoon (top) rein to give extra grip in the wet. Rubber covered reins can leave little rub marks on the horse's neck and give too much bulk. Be careful that your reins are wide enough, even if you are showing a hack in a lighter weight bridle. Many judges dislike 'shoelace reins' of very thin leather.

Bits

Before you even start thinking of what bit to use on your horse, make sure that his mouth and teeth are in good condition (as discussed in the previous chapter). It is also worth remembering that while different horses go better in different types of mouthpiece, a bit is only as kind or effective as the hands on the reins. Any mouthpiece is potentially severe in the hands of a rough rider.

Most textbooks will tell you that a thick mouthpiece is milder than a thinner one. In theory, that might be true – but it does not take into account the fact that horses have different shaped mouths and jaws. It is also often said that every horse should go best in a thick, single-jointed snaffle, but this again is not strictly true. Some horses do not like a single-jointed mouthpiece and are happier with an unjointed one or a French link mouthpiece, which has a kidney-shaped plate in the centre.

It is common sense to say that bits must fit properly, but go to any show and you will see that this is not always the case. Many people use bits that are too big; you should not be able to fit more than the width of your little finger between the bit rings and the corner of the horse's mouth. If there is any more leeway, a jointed bit will hang too low in the centre and the horse will be encouraged to put his tongue over it – any less and the rings may pinch the mouth. The bit should be just high enough to wrinkle the corners of the mouth.

Some of the bits from show producer Lynn Russell's collection. On the left is a double bridle, then clockwise from top are a Hanoverian pelham with Rugby cheeks; Rugby mullen-mouthed pelham; Hanoverian pelham; vulcanite mullen-mouthed pelham and jointed pelham.

Stainless steel is the most usual material for bit mouthpieces, but there are many others that can be considered if necessary. Copper encourages a horse to salivate, so a copper-covered mouthpiece or one which incorporates one or several copper rollers may be useful with a dry-mouthed animal. German steel has a higher copper content than that used in this country, and imported bits are now widely available. This kind of steel has a distinct yellow gold tinge, similar to nickel but not to be confused with it (nickel bends and can break).

Some horses do not like the feel or taste of cold steel, and could be tried in a bit with a hardened rubber (vulcanite) or ordinary rubber mouthpiece. German Nathe bits, available in most British saddlery shops through the distributors, Hydrophane, have white plastic mouthpieces that are flexible but strong and are also said to encourage salivation. A wet mouth is a potentially sensitive one, but a dry mouth has less feeling and is more likely to get bruised.

The type of curb chain used affects the strength of a bit's action. A plain, double link stainless steel curb chain is always correct, but light-mouthed or young horses may go better with a rubber sleeve over the chain or even a leather or elastic curb 'chain.' Whatever sort you choose, it is correct to use a leather lipstrap. This helps to ensure that the curb chain stays in the correct place and acts on the curb groove.

Whatever tack you use to school in at home, you should use a double bridle or some form of pelham for show classes. The double bridle is the classic bitting arrangement for hunters and cobs, and at one time no one would think of hunting in anything other than a double. The bits need to be of a good weight and not too short in the shank; usually you are better off with a sliding cheek rather than a fixed cheek Weymouth (curb). Hacks should go in a lighter weight, fixed cheek double with shorter shanks, such as the Tom thumb. Riding horses can go either way, but the bits should tend more towards the hunter weight.

If a horse does not like a double bridle, perhaps because his mouth is too short to accommodate the two bits comfortably, use some sort of pelham. A pelham is correct for all showing classes if necessary; there is a common and mistaken belief that it is more severe than a snaffle, but in many cases it can be milder. The majority of horses go better in a straight bar or mullen (half-moon) mouthpiece than a jointed one, and the simple reason that many horses are easier to ride in a pelham than a snaffle is that they are more comfortable and so resist the rider's hand less.

The SM and Hanoverian pelhams are less well known, but very useful bits. The SM is named after its inventor, Sam Marsh, and in the right hands is effective as well as being fairly mild. Its effectiveness stems from the hinged sides, which give independent rein action, and a mouthpiece which leaves room for the tongue and stays at the correct angle however the horse holds his head. The Hanoverian pelham has a roller (usually made from copper) set into the mouthpiece and discourages horses from rolling their tongues up. Young horses often accept it well.

You can give a more finished appearance to the horse's head by attaching a sliphead to the top bit ring. This is especially effective with a Rugby pelham, which has a separate loose ring.

Saddles

The first step in choosing a show saddle is to stand back and assess your horse's conformation. If he is a little short of front, put the saddle a little further back than usual; this makes him look more in proportion, and the adjustment is so slight that there is no danger of the saddle pressing on the loins.

A saddle should sit well on the horse's back, not look as if it is perched on top, and should be comfortable for both horse and rider. Avoid those with high pommels and cantles – look for a broad, flattish seat and broad panels that spread the weight over a wide area. Too many modern saddles have narrow panels that concentrate the rider's weight on small areas, leading to pressure points and sore backs.

Remember that judges are going to ride your horse, and no matter how well he goes, they will not be impressed if your tack is uncomfortable. If you are small and slim, remember that not all judges fit the same description! A judge with generous proportions will not enjoy riding on a saddle whose seat does not accommodate his own. The golden rule is that a small person can ride on a saddle that is a bit too big, but a large rider cannot manage with a saddle that is too small. If necessary, use a saddle that is a bit big for you when competing.

The same considerations apply to stirrup leathers and irons. Leathers must be long enough to suit long-legged judges and irons must be wide enough and deep enough – lady riders often forget that male judges sometimes have big feet, and trying to cram a size ten boot into an iron designed for a size five is uncomfortable and dangerous.

Your saddle should show off your horse's shoulder, not cover it up, so should not be too forward cut. Nor should it go to the other extreme and be too straight: you are looking for a happy medium with not too much knee or thigh roll. Some hack and riding horse exhibitors go for dressage-type saddles, but pure dressage saddles do not really belong in the show ring. Nor do dressage girths, as they tend to cover up the horse's elbow and can restrict his movement.

Professional exhibitors like reversed hide (suede) saddles. Old examples of these are much prized, and anyone who owns one will be reluctant to part with it. Professional exhibitors will happily pay as much for an old saddle by a maker such as Owen, as long as it is comfortable, as for a new one by a modern manufacturer. The same goes for side-saddles, which are dealt with in detail in Chapter 12. In a working hunter class, you may have to jump a decent track and need a saddle that you can ride effectively in. But as you are not allowed to change tack between the jumping section and the ride and conformation section, you have to be careful that it looks good on the horse. It may well be more forward-cut than a straight show saddle, but this should not be exaggerated.

Girths for all classes should be leather ones, either three-fold, Balding or Atherstone. Strictly speaking, you should not use a numnah, as it spoils the overall picture and your saddle should fit well without one. If a sensitive or cold-backed horse needs something between his back and the saddle, pick a numnah that is the same colour as your saddle and

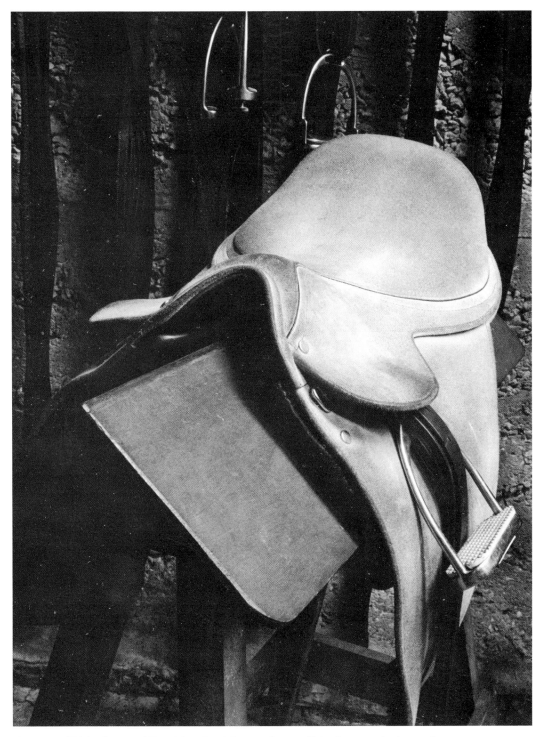

A reversed hide show saddle with a flattish seat shows off the horse to its best advantage.

does not show more than necessary – no fluffy monstrosities, please! A small piece of sheepskin, cut to fit your saddle, can also be useful; if you soap the underside of the saddle the sheepskin will not slip. Gel pads can be excellent, and are usually unobtrusive.

Care of tack

Good quality tack – which is the only sort you should consider using – is expensive. Treat it as an investment and look after it, even if cleaning tack does not come high on your list of favourite occupations.

If you want to save time and money, it can be worth using synthetic tack for everyday and saving your good quality leather saddlery for the show ring. Synthetic saddles, especially the latest Wintec and Thorowgood ranges, have come a long way since the early examples and designs are much better both in terms of fit and appearance. A general purpose saddle can be bought for a third of the price of a leather one and is lightweight and easy to look after; all you have to do is wipe it over with a damp cloth or, if necessary, hose it down – remembering that if it gets very wet it will take some time to dry.

Synthetic bridles come in a variety of materials, but are not generally as good as saddles. Some designs are better than others, and you need to check wear and tear (especially on stitching) especially carefully. Using a thin cotton numnah under a synthetic saddle helps to absorb sweat and avoid static: bridles are more of a problem and can cause rubs, so should be chosen with care and used with caution.

Leather tack should be wiped over after use, whenever possible, and taken apart and cleaned regularly. Use a glycerine saddle soap but never boot polish – you might get a desirable shine, but you will also end up with hard, slippery leather. New tack needs to be made supple before using it in the ring. This is particularly important with reins, and new pairs should be 'lasted,' a technique used in the Royal Mews. Hang them up, soap them, and knead them between your fingers for a few days before you ride with them, using a little fine leather oil.

The best way to put a shine on stainless steel bits and stirrup irons is to wash them in hot water and dry them off immediately with a soft cloth.

Clothes

You should be as smart and well-equipped as your horse. Different classes have different requirements, which can make them a sartorial minefield, but the most important thing to remember is that you are showing your horse, not your tastes in fashion. As with tack, it is always a good investment to buy the best quality riding clothes you can afford – they will fit better and last longer. If money is tight, it is worth considering good secondhand jackets and boots rather than new, inferior quality ones; look for advertisements in equestrian magazines and saddlers' shops or try specialist agencies.

Starting at the top, you need the correct headgear. Many shows now stipulate that this must meet British Standard Institution 6473 or 4472, so if in doubt, check. These hats have a three-point harness that is safe but not exactly elegant, but the best ones have flesh-coloured leather harnesses that are less obtrusive than dark nylon ones, common on cheaper models. Different styles suit different head shapes, so try several; you do not want to look as if you have a chimney stuck on top of your head.

Headgear to British Standards 4472 or 6473 must be worn for the jumping phase of working hunter classes, so you can choose between a skull cap and dark silk and a BS velvet-covered cap. For straight showing classes, velvet-covered caps are more in keeping. Some men prefer bowlers, especially for hunter and cob classes – the safety issue is one that comes down to personal choice, except when show rules state otherwise.

Jackets can make or mar your overall appearance. If you can only afford one, make it a good quality tweed that fits well. It should be long enough to cover your seat and should fit well at the shoulders and (for ladies) at the waist. Loud checks are inappropriate. Tweed jackets are correct for all hunter, cob and riding horse classes and for men showing hacks. Ladies usually wear solid colours (navy or black) for hack classes. Whatever you choose, avoid floral decorations in your buttonhole that make you look as if you have just come from a wedding.

Ladies and men wear shirts and ties, and colours for both are a matter of personal taste. If in doubt, be discreet – but if you prefer a pastel-coloured shirt and spotted or striped tie, why not? Ladies will find that men's or boy's shirts with structured collars are neater than blouses.

You cannot go wrong with beige or canary breeches, but white is inappropriate. Well-fitting leather boots are always preferable if you can afford them, and if you look after them will last for years. Made-to-measure ones are the ultimate, but not everyone's bank balance can meet their price tags.

Off the peg leather boots can usually be bought fairly reasonably, but if money is a problem there is nothing wrong with good quality rubber ones for local shows. Give them a more upmarket look by asking your saddler to sew leather garter straps on; these are a legacy of the days when breeches fastened at the knee with buttons rather than Velcro, and garter straps stopped them twisting round and pressing into the leg.

Spurs are correct for all showing classes (though judges do not wear them). If your horse is very sharp, or you do not feel happy wearing them, choose ones with very short shanks or even 'dummy' spurs with no shank at all. Make sure they fit correctly on the boot seam: too many riders wear them low down on the heel instead of on the ankle.

You should always wear gloves and carry a whip. Gloves should be brown leather (not black or navy) and your cane should be malacca or leather covered. Cutting whips can be carried in working hunter classes, but if you feel you might need to hit your horse the chances are that you should not have entered the class.

If you qualify for one of the evening performances at Wembley, the price of fame is some substantial investment in special togs. Men wear black or pink hunting coats; if the latter, white breeches and boots with tops and white garter straps must go with them. Black coats can be worn with white breeches and top boots or coloured (beige or canary) with plain black boots. Ladies wear black or blue jackets with beige or canary breeches, black boots and garter straps. Men must wear top hats, and some ladies now choose them as well.

Chapter 10
Trimming and Presentation

A good-looking horse can be made to look even better with clever trimming and plaiting. Although nothing can make a horse with bad conformation into a show animal, the right presentation can turn what at first sight looks like an ugly duckling into a swan. There are many ways in which you can minimise small faults by clever turnout techniques, such as the way you plait a mane.

Start by standing back and taking a long, hard look at your horse – something you need to do regularly as a matter of course. Is he in good condition, or is he too thin or too fat? A show horse should be well rounded, but not fat; you see too many hunters that are so gross they cannot gallop, and too many cobs with pads of fat on the crest of the neck and shoulders. If you are feeding your horse correctly, he will be feeling well in himself, and that will show in a bright eye, shiny coat and general interest in life.

A shiny coat starts in the feed room, so check your horse's diet against his appearance and the way he is going. There is an old saying that 'It's not what you do to the outside that counts but what you put on the inside' – in other words, a balanced diet counts for a lot more than hours of grooming.

Before you start trimming and pulling, check the rules for your particular class – for instance, you would pull and plait the mane of a part-bred Arab, but not a pure-bred. Then prepare to work miracles, because a pair of clippers and a pulling comb can transform the hairiest monster into a picture of elegance. Whether you are preparing a hack or a cob, the basic aim is the same: a sharp outline that shows off the horse to its best advantage, with no fuzzy edges such as hairy heels or jawlines.

Trimming

A pair of electric or battery-operated clippers with fine or medium blades is suitable for all trimming jobs. Some horses dislike having their heads clipped at first, and it is safer to use a twitch than risk being pinned against a stable wall by a 17.2hh heavyweight who takes an exception to being smartened up.

Some people dislike the idea of using a twitch, which holds the top lip tight, but as long as it is correctly applied the horse is not, as is commonly supposed, in pain. In fact, the latest research shows that twitching a horse stimulates the production of natural substances in the body called endorphins, which give him a feeling of relaxation and well-being.

Logic will tell you that this must be true – if you inflict pain on a horse he will fight you, but horses that are twitched inevitably stand quietly and even doze.

The most basic kind of twitch is a short length of broom handle with a loop of string at one end, which is twisted round the horse's top lip. This is nowhere near as good or as kind in its action as the specially-made metal humane twitch, which looks like a large pair of nutcrackers and can be bought from most saddlers. Inevitably, there will be the odd occasion when a twitch is not enough – in this case, ask your vet about tranquillising the horse to enable you to clip in safety.

Trimming is a matter of technique. Starting at the head, close the horse's ears gently in your hand and trim down the outside. This gives the sharp outline we are looking for, but leaves enough protection on the inside against insects and seeds which may fall into the ears.

Which cob came third at Wembley at his first attempt? Believe it or not, it was Orbit, the hairy one on the left. This shows what a difference clippers can make in skilled hands.

The debate on whether or not to trim off whiskers is a perennial one. Some people believe that they act as feelers and as such should be left on, but they are always removed for top level showing. Watching horses out in the fields, they certainly do not seem to suffer from losing their whiskers and search the pasture just as efficiently. At the end of the day, it is up to you – but you will have to accept that a bewhiskered horse will probably stand out like a sore thumb in a showing line-up.

Unless your horse has a sparse mane, when you need all the hair you can get to plait, it looks neatest if you clip out a short section where the bridle headpiece goes. Be very careful: do not clip out more than about one to one and a half inches, or you will have one fewer plait and give the unwanted optical illusion that your horse is shorter in the neck than he actually is. Be equally careful at the withers – nothing looks worse than big gaps left by the clippers, and again, it is too easy to make the horse's neck look shorter.

If your horse is a little thick in the jowl, run the clippers along the underside of the jaw. This will give a cleaner outline; as with so many trimming techniques, a couple of minutes' work can make an enormous difference. Cobs in particular are very rewarding to trim if you know what you are doing, and you can produce some amazing 'befores' and 'afters'.

Legs should also be tidied up. If the horse is fine boned, use the clippers going down in the direction of the coat. For a coarser cob with full feathers on its heels, clip against the lie of the hair for a sharper finish. You will also need to trim the ergots; the easiest way to do this is with a pair of secateurs, but be careful not to cut them too close.

Finally, trim round the top of the coronets. Use scissors on fine hair and small clipper blades on coarse, and hold them on a slant to get a neat finish. This is one of those tiny finishing touches that makes all the difference.

Manes and tails

Unless your horse is shown unplaited, you will need to pull his mane and tail. If you particularly want to leave a full tail and plait it for shows, there is nothing to stop you doing so – but unfortunately it is one of the things that will make you stand out as an amateur in a professional line-up. Professionals always pull tails rather than plaiting them, because it is quicker and does not weaken the tail hair as frequent plaiting would.

The tail should be banged (cut straight across at the bottom) and kept short enough. Nothing looks worse than a tail hanging round a horse's fetlocks; the correct length is between two and four inches below the point of the hocks when the horse is moving, so you will need to see him led out in hand to judge how he carries his tail naturally. You can then ask an assistant to hold the tail at the appropriate angle while you shorten it or, if you have to manage alone (and the horse is quiet enough) put a stick under the dock. Hold the tail hairs tightly together and cut straight across. Using a clipper blade rather than a pair of scissors enables you to get a nice straight edge rather than 'steps'.

Pulling a tail well takes practice and experience, and the best way to learn is to ask someone knowledgeable to demonstrate it to you. Some are easier than others; the worst of all is a horse with a fat dock and coarse tail hair. In theory you should only take hair from the sides, but in cases like this you might have to take a little from the middle and top. Use a short-toothed pulling comb or an ordinary plastic comb (the sort sold for people rather than horses) cut to a suitable length, whatever you find easiest.

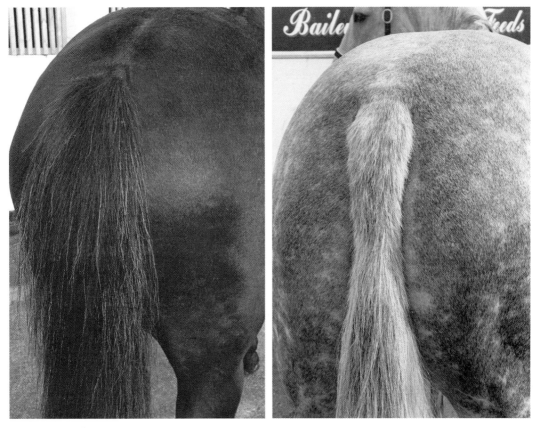

Left: An unpulled tail and (right) one which has been pulled and bandaged.

Wind the hair round the comb, taking just a few hairs at a time, and pull them out in a quick, sharp motion. Some people like to protect the skin on the inside of the finger joints by wrapping sticking plaster round, but this is not usually necessary if you use a comb. Try to pull manes and tails when the horse is warm (such as after exercise) as the pores are open and the hair comes out much more easily. If you are in any doubt about the horse's reaction to having his tail done, stand straw bales behind him in the stable. That way they get kicked rather than you.

Once a tail is pulled, putting a tail bandage on for a couple of hours a day will help to keep it in shape. As the hair starts to grow out, use a small pair of pliers to grip and pull the short hairs that you cannot get out with your fingers and comb.

If you are committed to a full tail, be prepared to spend time plaiting it for every show. Again, the best way to learn is to get an expert to show you: the commonest mistakes are to take too much hair to start off the plait and not keeping it tight enough as you work down the dock. You will need to bandage your horse's tail for travelling, but do not pull off the bandage as you would normally or all your hard work will be undone. Undo the tapes and unwind the bandage.

Pulling manes is a lot easier than pulling tails. The trick is to remember that you are pulling to achieve the correct thickness rather than the correct length – if you carry on pulling an already fine mane you will end up with a wispy, straggling mess. Once you have achieved the correct thickness, use an old clipper blade or one from a broken pair to shorten it: take a lock of hair at a time, pull it taut and slice down with the blade. This gives a neat but natural look and avoids the artificial 'cut' look that you always get by using scissors. It is especially useful on horses with long but fine manes, as is the case with many Thoroughbreds, when pulling would leave too little hair to plait.

Pull a mane from underneath to get the required thickness.

If a mane has been well pulled, it will be a lot easier to plait. Plaiting a newly-washed mane is difficult, as the clean hair is slippery and hard to get hold of, so try and give it a couple of days after washing to settle down – otherwise it is a bit like the old television advert, 'just washed it and can't do a thing with it'.

Tradition used to dictate that horses should have either seven or nine plaits, but that has more or less died out. It is really up to you to decide how many look best, with the proviso that too many small ones look silly. Plaits bound with white tape, as are fashionable in some dressage circles, are definitely not for the show ring – and unless you have a dire emergency, neither are ones secured with rubber bands.

Use a spare clipper blade to shorten it without giving a 'cut' look.

Step-by-step to plaiting a mane. These are set on top of the neck.

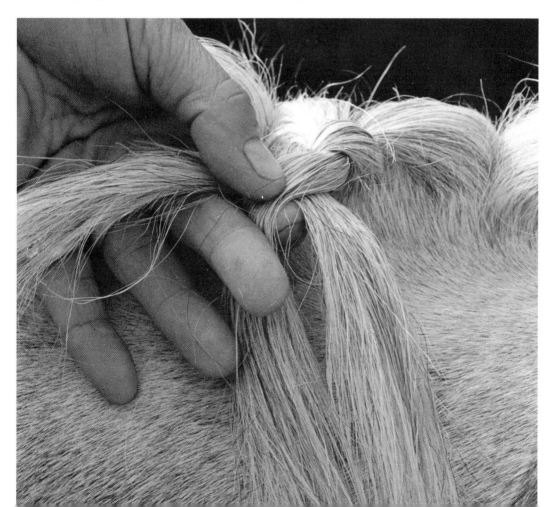

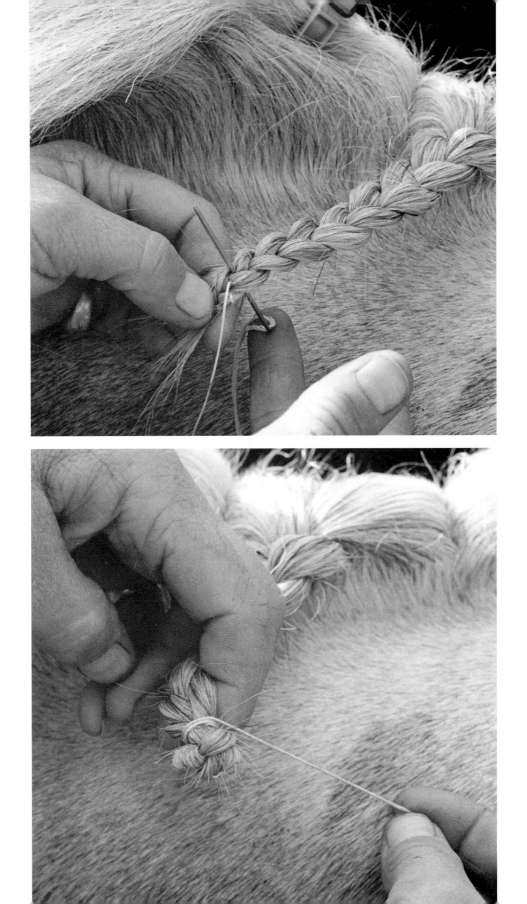

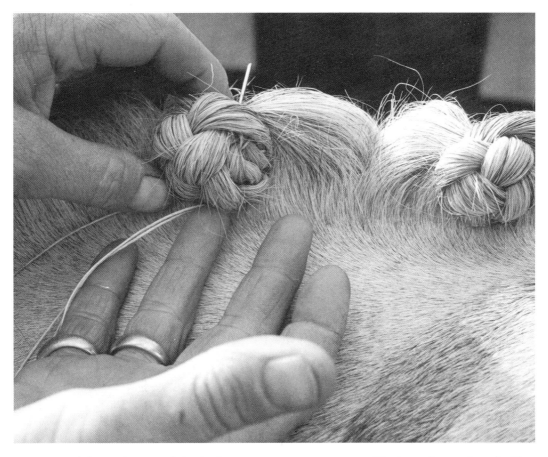

Fewer plaits make a neck look shorter; more can create an illusion of extra length. You also need to decide how to position the plaits. If the horse has a weak top line, set them on top of the neck to give the impression of more bulk; if his neck is too heavy, set them to the side.

Comb the mane through and spray hair gel – the sort made for human use – across the top, shielding the neck with your other hand to stop the gel falling on the coat and making it sticky. You will find that the gel helps you keep the hair together, rather than getting odd little wisps sticking up round the plaits.

Keep the plaits tight from the base, fasten at the end, roll up and stitch. If you want them to sit on top of the neck, push back as you stitch. Some people are naturally deft and find plaiting easy, while others feel as if they have two left hands. But it really is one of those things where practice makes perfect, and eventually you should be able to plait a mane in 20 minutes to half an hour.

It is very important not to damage the hair when you unpick the plaits, especially if you are showing most weekends. A dressmaker's stitch unpicker is easier to use than scissors and is much kinder to the hair.

Cobs are in one respect a lot easier to get ready for a show than other horses – their hogged manes mean you do not have to plait. Hogging is done quickly and easily with clippers, though you have to be careful not to cut into the neck hair. If your cob has a strong neck, hog him the day before a show, but if he is slightly weak in this area then hog about a week before he is due to go in the ring. This allows for a slight growth, which will give the impression of a better neck.

Bathing

It used to be said that too much bathing was bad for horses. They used to say that about people, too! Obviously it does not make sense to strip the natural oils out of a coat and then replace them with artificial spray-on coat sheens, but there is no reason why a show horse cannot be as clean as his owner. Grease and dust dull the coat, and while a grass-kept pony needs a woolly coat and plenty of grease as protection against the weather, the same cannot be said for a show horse.

Within reason, you can bath a horse at any time, though it would not be very kind to do it when it is bitterly cold and a freezing wind is blowing. Ideally, you should bath the horse one or two days before a show, to give the coat time to flatten down again; if you have a grey who manages to put stable stains where other horses did not know they could exist, you will need to keep him covered up with a cotton summer sheet and hood and do some 'spot washing' on the morning of the show, if necessary.

You want to get the job over and done with as quickly and efficiently as possible, so get everything ready before you start and, if possible, use warm water. In hot weather you can wash the whole horse in one go, but otherwise it is kindest to do an equine strip wash. Start by doing the head, neck and front, then fold a rug over his front end while you do the back one. Be careful to rinse out all the shampoo, as any traces left will dull the coat and defeat the object.

As soon as you have finished, rug him up well if necessary and walk him round to dry off. Some yards, usually racing ones, have special washing and drying stables with infra-red lamps suspended from the ceilings – the rest of us have to make do with rugs. This is where modern high-tech materials are a bonus, such as Thermatex rugs or ones with Flectalon linings. These can be put straight on to a wet horse and keep him dry while the moisture is transferred to the outer surface of the rug.

Coat gloss can give a finishing touch, and is especially useful when you have just given your horse a bath. Applied to the damp coat after he has been rinsed and sweat scraped, it will help repel dirt and dust. Coat gloss also helps keep manes and tails in good condition; it helps prevent the hairs tangling and means you can separate them with your fingers rather than using a brush.

White leg markings are very attractive, and can help your horse catch the judge's eye if there are fourteen bay geldings in the ring and he is the only one with any white on him.

White socks can also be a nuisance, as they quickly become dirty. Purely as a cosmetic touch, you can apply white chalk to brighten them – but only on bone dry hair and only on the day of the show. Hoof oil gives the final finishing touch before you go in the ring.

Chapter 11
The Show

Early shows are inevitably full of distractions and excitement for young and novice horses. The most sensible introduction to this new experience is to pick one or two small but well-run local shows and treat them as schooling outings – take your horse along purely for the experience, if possible with a helper who has plenty of common sense and an older horse who knows the ropes. This way your novice will get used to all the sights and sounds, and if he is going to get carried away with it you can find somewhere to work him that will not get in other exhibitors' way. It also saves you the embarrassment of being bucked off in front of a judge.

You cannot predict exactly how a horse is going to behave at his early shows: some will surprise you and accept everything that is going on as a matter of course, and some who are normally quiet will temporarily turn into equine Jekyll and Hydes. This is where the rider's experience counts; professionals know when to be calm and tactful and when to be firm. There are times when a soothing word and a reassuring pat on the neck are the best approach – and others when a sharp slap is called for. Hopefully you will know your horse well enough to be able to distinguish between excitement and naughtiness, and react accordingly.

Preparations for and the actual journey to the show are as important as what happens when you get there. Show horses need to be good travellers, and if a horse is a bad traveller, then ninety-nine times out of a hundred it is bad handling that has caused this. The basics are the same, whether you are travelling him in a luxury lorry or a trailer and tow vehicle – he must be well equipped, well handled and transported by a careful driver.

Protective travelling gear is essential, no matter how short your journey. The horse's most vulnerable areas are limbs, poll and dock, which should all be protected from possible injury, and you also need to make sure that he is rugged correctly.

Starting at the top, you should always travel (or turn out) a horse in a leather headcollar rather than a nylon one. The reason for this is that if he panics or gets caught up, leather will break: nylon may not, but there is a good chance that his neck will. If he is a big horse or tends to throw his head up, you will need to fit a poll guard. There are several designs available, and if you choose one with earholes you need to make sure they are large enough. Pollguards and browbands that pinch the ears will irritate the horse and he may throw his head up or scratch it on projections in the horsebox, risking injury.

Whether you use bandages and padding or travelling boots is a matter of personal choice. Boots are quicker to put on and take off, but bandages give better protection and

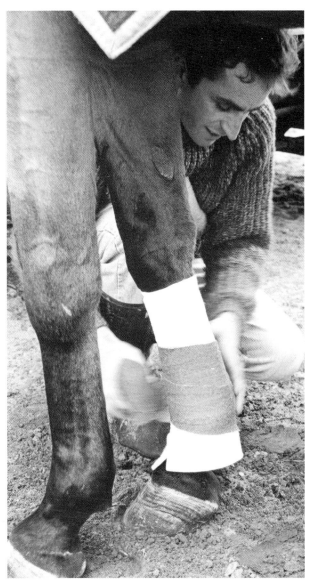

Bandages over padding are usually preferable to travelling boots.

are less likely to slip or rub. There are some well designed (and expensive) travelling boots on the market, but there are many more not so well designed ones. If they are perfectly in proportion to your horse's leg, boots may be perfectly all right; if not, they may slip.

Some people worry that they may put travelling bandages on too tight. As long as you use padding such as Fybagee, Gamgee or cotton bandage quilts underneath the risk of this happening is unlikely. All you have to do is keep the tension of the bandages even and if they fasten with tie tapes, tie them so the knot is on the side of the neck and not at the back (where it can damage the tendon) or at the front (where it may press on the cannon bone).

Another frequently heard reason for not using bandages is that it is difficult to take them off a young horse who comes off the lorry dancing with excitement. The answer in this case is to tape over the fastenings for extra security, ensuring that the tape is no tighter than the bandage, and leave them on until the horse has been ridden in and has calmed down. They provide valuable protection while you are warming up, and it means you can get tacked up and straight on with the job instead of fiddling around; once the horse's mind is on his job and his brain is back between his ears, you will be able to take them off without any problem.

Some people like to use knee and hock boots, but these have the top straps fastened so tightly there is a danger of rubbing. There may be times when you feel they are called for, if you are unfortunate enough to have a horse who persistently kicks out or bangs his front legs on the vehicle, but usually they are not essential. In any case, a horse who behaves in such a bad mannered way should be left in no doubt that it is not acceptable. The vulnerable coronet area can be protected by using overreach boots in front and behind – this also minimises the risk of horses treading on and pulling off their shoes.

Tail bandages are essential to protect the dock. Big horses often sit back, and the tail hair is easily rubbed and broken – in this case, it is a good idea to put on your tail bandage, wrap bandage padding round and put a second bandage over the top. If you want to keep the long tail hair clean, especially with grey horses, add a second bandage below the first or put an old stocking over the horse's tail and bandage over the top.

The rugs you use will depend on the weather and the ventilation in your vehicle. Horses need to be warm and protected from draughts, but not too hot. In summer a simple cotton sheet may suffice, but if the weather turns colder your horse will need extra warmth. There are now some very good lightweight rugs with thermal properties that double as anti-sweat rugs by wicking with the moisture being transmitted through the rug to the outer surface. As our climate is unpredictable, it is always better to be prepared for any eventuality and take too many rugs rather than too few.

Always allow yourself plenty of time for the journey. If you are in a hurry and start hustling your horse up the ramp and then have to drive faster than you really want to, your horse will probably arrive anxious and sweating. Even if you are in time for your class, neither of you will be in the state of mind to perform well.

Driving skills are paramount. If you are not a hundred per cent certain that you can give the horse a smooth ride, hire a professional transporter until you have learned the necessary skills. There are several companies who specialise in intensive driving and towing courses – look for advertisements in the leading equestrian magazines.

If your horse is difficult or reluctant to load, get expert advice. There are all sorts of reasons why horses become bad loaders; often it is because they are asked to go into a badly lit vehicle, so they cannot see where they are going, or they have been travelled with the partitions in too tight.

The latter is too often the case with trailers: remember that a horse needs to spread his feet to balance himself, so the first thing to do if he travels badly is to give him more room, not less. People often move the partitions in 'to give him more support', but this is the worst thing you can do. You may have to take the central partition out of a trailer altogether if you are travelling a big horse.

At the show

As your first couple of shows are simply schooling outings, tack up your horse and ride him round the quieter parts of the showground. If he comes down the ramp looking a hand bigger than normal and with his eyes on stalks, and your instinct for self preservation triumphs over your desire to ride him, you may be tempted to lunge him for a few minutes first.

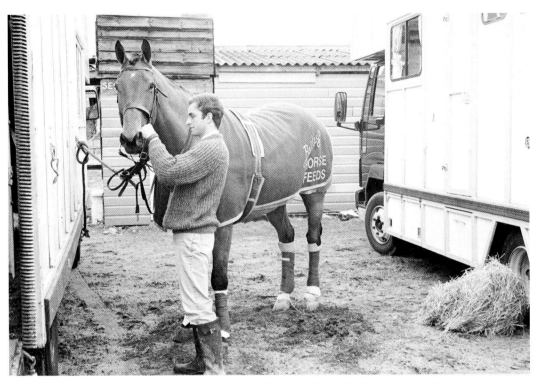

Early shows teach horses attributes such as standing quietly while they are tacked up.

If you do, pick a corner of the showground where you will not get in anyone else's way and make sure your horse is under control. This means lungeing off the bit rather than from a headcollar or lungeing cavesson – we are talking essential control rather than finesse. As soon as he has got his initial excitement out of his system, get on: lungeing for hours on end will simply tire him out, and you want to be able to work him properly.

Find a quiet corner to ride round rather than putting him straight into the middle of all the hustle and bustle. Keep him going forwards and try and establish right from the start that he must listen to you – do not force him into an outline and take a heavy hand, but on the other hand do not let him walk round listening to everything but your aids. No matter how many distractions there are, you should still expect him to stop and start when you want him to and go at the pace you ask.

No matter how big or small the show, you will need eyes in the back of your head and the sixth sense to judge what the idiot in front of you is going to do just before he or she does it. Watch out for children zooming around on ponies and people who suddenly fire horses over practice jumps from a standstill.

As your horse starts to settle, you can show him a few of the sights. Let him look at the trade stands and the ice cream vans, and make him stand for a short time while you chat with a friend. While you will be ready to make allowance for new distractions, you should never be prepared to forego basic good manners.

It should not take more than one or two outings before your horse is ready to compete. Two classes per show are plenty for a novice horse in his first season, so do not overdo it even if he behaves perfectly. In fact, two classes per show is usually plenty even for an experienced horse; you may occasionally do three, but it will be the exception rather than the rule.

No matter what your horse's type, you should have plenty of choice. Many small shows now run ring experience classes designed to introduce young horses to competition; these can be very useful provided you accept that you may have a collection of novices trotting round the ring, and it only takes one to spook and set off the whole lot.

Ride a young or novice horse round and show him the sights. Here Mercury's travelling bandages have been left on deliberately for protection.

If you are entering an open class, perhaps for riding or riding club horses, you obviously have to accept that you will be competing against more experienced animals . . . though there is no reason why a nice, well-schooled novice cannot compete on equal terms. Many

Your horse must listen to you when being worked in company. Pluto is experienced and not bothered by crowds; a novice would have been worked alone in a quiet spot first.

shows run novice as well as open classes, but be careful about working hunter classes and be prepared to withdraw if the course is more difficult than you feel confident of tackling. Most novice working hunter courses are and should be straightforward and inviting, but you get the occasional one that is badly designed with awkward distances between the fences.

Once you get into the show routine, preparations will become second nature. The horse should be bathed and trimmed up a couple of days before, and cotton sheets and if necessary hoods will help keep him clean at night. On the actual morning of the show you will need to plait up (unless you are showing a cob, whose hogged mane relieves you of that task and may sometimes seem a good enough reason for buying one!).

Aim to arrive so that you have plenty of time before your first class. Send your helper (essential for early shows and just as welcome at later ones) to collect your number, if necessary, and to check whether the schedule is running to time. You will have to time your working-in according to your horse's temperament: you want him alert and listening, but not over the top or so tired he has lost all his sparkle.

Remember that you are out to make a good impression from the moment you enter the ring, so keep your wits about you. Your horse should be going forward in a round outline, not slopping along on a loose rein gazing at the scenery. Even if the judge is conferring with a steward or has not actually arrived in the ring, you should be getting on with the job. If the judge glances up and sees your horse mooching along like a giraffe, it will not exactly strike the right note.

Walking the course for a working hunter or cob class demands concentration.

One of the essential attributes for showing is to develop eyes in the back of your head. You need to be aware not only what you are asking your horse to do, but what other competitors are doing as well. Unfortunately, some of them may not always be too sure, especially in novice classes. You will soon spot the people who are having problems or do not realise that they are crowding others – keep out of their way.

Create your own space in the ring, and if necessary circle inside to make some more rather than get too close to another horse. This can also be a judicious manoeuvre if someone persists in getting too close to you, coupled with a polite request that he or she keeps a reasonable distance. If necessary, warn that your horse may kick if crowded, even if you are pretty sure that this is not the case.

Keep enough distance between you and the horse in front.

You can never be sure exactly when the judge will turn to look at you, so assume that you are under scrutiny all the time. Be alert for instructions from the steward, who will tell you when to move up from one pace to another, when to change the rein and so on. As soon as you know what you need to do next, pick the right place and prepare your horse. For instance, if you are told to canter on, wait until you reach the next corner and ask the horse to strike off as you come out of it. This way you can rebalance the horse, get the correct bend and stand a much better chance of getting a smooth, correct strike-off.

Some people unfortunately think that clever ringcraft means cutting in front of fellow competitors as they go past the judge. The judge will not be impressed; this is the height of bad manners and something you should always try to avoid.

Inevitably, there will be times when things do not go quite right. Your horse may strike off on the wrong canter lead, or even throw a buck. If things go wrong, the golden rule is 'Smile – and don't panic!' In the case of the wrong canter lead, bring the horse back to trot and ask again when you have established rhythm and bend; if possible, wait until the next corner. If your horse bucks or lights up because he is excited at cantering in company,

Keep one eye on the judge and his steward, the other on fellow competitors – and the one in the back of your head on everything else!

circle to the inside and create some space. The only consolation is that it happens to everyone at some time or other.

If you are asked to gallop, you will need to take the size of the ring and the class into account. Remember that you do not want to hurtle flat out round the ring; you are aiming to set up the horse in the corner and ask him to lengthen down the long side. Obviously you need space to do this, so keep your distance from the horse in front as you make your preparations.

The judge will want to ride your horse and assess his conformation; some larger shows have individual judges for each of these phases. For the conformation phase, your helper will remove the horse's saddle and, if possible, brush off sweat marks. You do not need to launch into a full blown grooming session, complete with hoof oil, in the middle of the ring: a quick tidy up is all that is needed.

Stand the horse up so that the judge can see how he is made. The horse should be alert and interested, not resting his hindleg and using this phase as an excuse for a quiet doze. Some people pick grass to get the horse's attention, but a nice rustling paper bag in your pocket often has a better effect.

Practise at home until your horse trots up willingly in front of the judge.

When the judge has looked the horse over he will ask you to walk away and trot back. Practice at home should mean that the horse knows exactly what to do, but some get very crafty and try and hang back. If you suspect that your horse might try this, get your helper to stand with a handkerchief or stable rubber and flick it discreetly at the horse as you turn him to trot him back (always turning him away from you). This, accompanied by a quiet click of the tongue, should do the trick. Keep it subtle, no waving arms or loud sound effects.

Watching the judge ride your horse can be very interesting. If you are fortunate enough to be pulled in top of the line, you can only keep your fingers crossed, but if he rides other horses before yours, notice how he handles them. Not all judges are brilliant riders, and one who takes too tight a hold on a sensitive horse might not get the smoothest of rides. It is always amusing to watch the hunter classes at county shows when a less than tactful judge gets on – as he rides the first horse round, you will see a surreptitious loosening of curb chains down the line.

Above: Make sure your tack is suitable for a judge who may be larger than you.

Below: The steward will call you into line, so be ready for his signal.

If the judge asks you about your horse, give a short but pleasant answer. He does not want a detailed history of his life, nor does he want to know how marvellous he is: he is there to find that out for himself. If the judge does not say anything, keep your own mouth shut except to smile and say 'thank you' when he hands the horse back to you.

There will always be times when you think that the judge has been hard on your horse. There may even be occasions when you think that he is a blind, unco-ordinated halfwit who should never be allowed to get on a horse. If so, keep your thoughts to yourself and keep smiling. By entering the class, you presented yourself and your horse for someone else's opinion – and if you do not like it, that is hard luck. There is always another day, another class and another judge.

Judges are only human, and different people like different types of horse. If you have a flashy chestnut and you learn after a few shows that a particular judge hates them, you are wasting your time exhibiting under that judge. In theory, judges should not have prejudices: in practice, some do, even if they are not aware of them! All you can do is resolve not to let your own prejudices cloud your judgement if you ever become a judge.

There will be times when you do not win and feel sure that you deserved to. They may even be times when you win and know that the horse did not go well enough to merit standing top of the line! Whatever happens, keep smiling and remember that you are out to enjoy yourself.

Chapter 12
Side-Saddle

Over the past few years side-saddle riding has enjoyed a boom in popularity. In many ways it is hardly surprising: nothing looks more elegant than a lady in a beautifully cut habit on a well-schooled horse, especially in the show ring.

To an inexperienced onlooker, side-saddle riding may look slightly precarious, but in fact you are probably more secure than when riding astride. It is often the answer for someone who has balance problems because of disability, and because it is easier to establish a secure seat you may find it easier to keep a light hand. To ride well side-saddle you have to sit straight, strange as that may sound! Anyone who rides reasonably well astride should find that they are getting the hang of things in about six weeks, though as with any skill, the more you find out the more you realise there is to learn.

The price of lessons varies, but will probably be about £20 an hour for private tuition. Many teachers will only teach people on their own horses, but you may be lucky enough to find someone who has a schoolmaster they will allow you to ride for your first few lessons. If you have to learn on your own horse, and he has never been ridden side-saddle before, make sure he is introduced to it by someone experienced. Most horses take to it quite kindly, but as with all aspects of training, you do not want the blind leading the blind.

The only time you would not be at least as safe as riding astride, if not safer, is on a horse that rears – which in any case is not a pleasant problem to deal with and should not be tackled by anyone but a professional who knows the risks and is prepared to take them. If a horse goes up and comes over backwards, the side-saddle may hold you in place so securely that the horse will fall on top of you.

You should also be careful about riding young horses side-saddle. Side-saddles are much heavier than ordinary ones, and the rider is required to sit on the horse's back much more, with less scope to redistribute her weight. A four-year-old is really too immature physically to cope with this: wait until he is at least five, and avoid any horse whose conformation predisposes him to back weaknesses, whatever his age.

The most important thing about choosing a horse for side-saddle is that he must have a reasonable front (in other words, that he has a nice sloping shoulder, is broad enough through the chest and has a good length of rein). He must have reasonable conformation and should hopefully not be too short coupled. Horses with short backs tend not be so comfortable; a slightly long back, as long as it is not so exaggerated as to be a weakness, is less of a drawback than normal as it gives more room for the side-saddle.

In theory you could compete side-saddle in any pure showing class; in practice, it tends to be restricted to specific classes for ladies' hunters, alongside the ones for ladies' hunters to be ridden astride. If you want to show your horse side-saddle in a class that is basically recognised as an astride one – such as a working hunter competition – you have to seek prior permission from the judge and make sure that you have an ordinary saddle available for him or her to ride on.

Showing classes are, of course, judged with the horse in mind. Side-saddle equitation classes are very different, and here it is the rider who is under scrutiny. Run under the auspices of the Side-Saddle Association, they provide valuable experience for anyone wanting to have a go in another sphere of riding. They also offer another showing avenue for the nice horse who does not quite fit in to a definite weight category – perhaps the hunter who falls between lightweight and middleweight, or the high class riding club horse who is half an inch over a height limit.

If you are interested in side-saddle riding, or want to find a good instructor, the Side-Saddle Association is the best place to start (see appendix of useful addresses). The association runs its own specialised show each year with side-saddle classes for cobs, hacks, hunters, riding horses and working hunters.

Turnout

Turnout is vitally important for all showing classes, and perhaps even more so for side-saddle ones. Side-saddle equitation classes have a special section where the turnout is taken into consideration, including the safety and suitability of the tack. The rider's habit is an essential ingredient of the overall picture, and must be well fitting and of the correct colour.

Your best bet is to look for an old, secondhand habit in good condition that fits you well or can be altered to fit. This will usually set you back about £200 to £250, which might sound a lot for a secondhand outfit – but the old ones are definitely the best ones! Look for names like Roberts and Carol and Cobb, via advertisements in magazines such as *Horse and Hound* and through the Side-Saddle Association. You can still get habits made to measure, but it is difficult to get cloth of such good quality. It is this quality that makes the all-important difference between a habit that hangs well and holds its shape and one that looks like a dishrag.

Remember that you want to present a picture of grace and elegance. This means that your jacket must fit at the waist and be long enough in the sleeves. It also means that the hem of your apron should be level and about two inches above the seam of your left boot – according to the SSA rule book, the right toe 'should *never* show under any circumstances'. It also means that when someone walks by they see your legs encased elegantly in the folds of your habit, not flashes of breeches because the apron is skimpily cut or does not hang properly. There is an old saying that 'It isn't what you wear, it's the way you wear it,' and to a certain extent that is true. It definitely helps if you have a slim figure, but you can still look elegant even if you have more statuesque proportions. It is what the old books used to call 'deportment', a way of sitting and carrying yourself that gives you an air of grace and confidence.

If you are working on a limited budget (which most of us are) then go for a navy or black habit. For most women, navy is softer and more flattering; black can look harsh. To be correct, you should wear a bowler, which must be set so that the brim is level – not set at a jaunty angle.

Other essentials are a veil and a bun. If your own hair is not long enough to form the real thing, which should be no bigger than a small doughnut, you will need to wear a false one: it is one of those quaint traditions that make side-saddle special! The veil should be a proper side-saddle veil which stretches neatly across the face without wrinkles and bags (even if there are a few underneath). Too many people think that a length of any old veiling material will do, pinned on any old how.

Things sometimes go wrong even for the best riders. Just keep smiling, and don't panic.

The hats issue is one which again comes down to personal choice. There is nothing to prevent you wearing a BSI standard velvet-covered cap for any side-saddle class, and in fact the Side-Saddle Association makes this compulsory for all junior riders (defined as aged under 16 on 1 January of the relevant year). But although the rule book makes it clear that anyone is entitled to wear a BSI standard 4472 or 6473 hat, and in theory you should not be marked down because of it, there is no way you will be placed in a *concours d'elegance.*

Your shirt should have a nicely-fitting collar and tie, complemented by a yellow, buff or Tattersall check waistcoat – avoid loud checks. Leather boots, with one blunt or dummy spur, brown leather gloves and a cane complete the picture. Side Saddle Association rules, which apply to equitation classes, say that a whip or rigid cane not more than one metre in length should be carried, and must be of sufficient length to be used as a right leg aid.

If you hit the heights and need a silk hat – traditionally worn only after mid-day at county shows and never for preliminary judging – you need to team it with a hunting tie or stock and stockpin and a red waistcoat. It is very difficult to find modern silk hats as good as the old ones: even the specialist hat makers say they simply cannot get silk of such good quality. So if you get the chance to beg, borrow or buy an old one in good condition, do not miss it. There is a definite distinction between a silk top hat and a dressage one, so do not pick the wrong one; the silk hat is taller.

If money is no object, you might like to wear a tweed habit for morning county show hunter classes. This should have a restrained check and be worn with long brown boots bowler, shirt and tie etc as before.

Saddles and bridles

Good side-saddles are worth their weight in gold, and as they are pretty heavy to start with this signifies a hefty investment. As with habits, the old ones are the best ones. If you can find a side-saddle by Owen, Champion and Wilton, Mayhew or Whippy you will be riding on the best; side-saddle making is an art in itself, and very few saddlers today could match the old craftsmen.

Price depends on condition, and a good show side-saddle will be £850 upwards. Good old side-saddles are like antiques, and will increase rather than decrease in value. One that is not in such top condition will cost anything from £400. Again, the Side-Saddle Association is the best starting point, and keeps lists of specialist saddlers and people who have side-saddles and habits for sale.

Buying and fitting side-saddles takes a lot of experience, so if you do not have it ask the advice of someone who has. As a basic first essential, make sure that any saddle you consider buying has a safety fitting, which will ensure that if you have a fall the leather will be released and you will not get dragged.

The construction of a side-saddle is different from that of an ordinary one. The tree of an ordinary saddle fits across the withers and is equally adjusted either side, but a side-

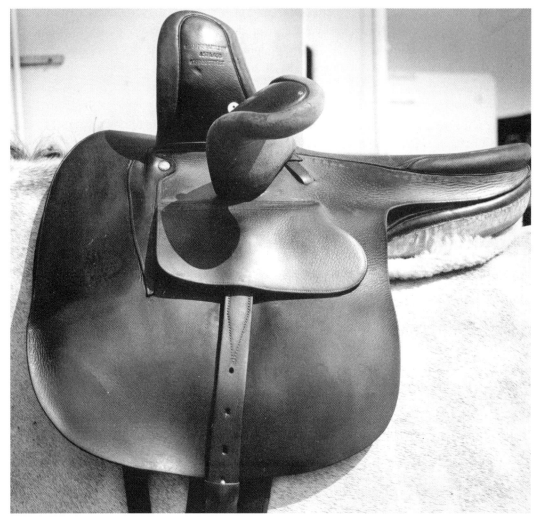

An old Champion and Wilton side-saddle, built with a craftsmanship it would be hard to find today.

saddle tree is longer on the near side than the off. This means it is unbalanced to start with – and then we add two pommels on the nearside and none on the other to unbalance it even further.

Most side-saddles weigh about two stones, which is a lot of extra weight for a horse to carry (and an extra incentive for any of the more statuesque side-saddle riders mentioned earlier to go on a diet). In the old days, they were custom-made for individual clients, and the saddler would take a range of body measurements. They were also made so that ladies who rode side-saddle every day could ride on the nearside and the offside, which it was believed help prevent curvature of the spine. It must certainly have helped the horses' backs, if not those of the riders.

A side-saddle has three straps: an ordinary girth, a balance girth and a safety one. Sometimes the feel of the balance strap, which as the name suggests is designed to keep the balance of the saddle equal on the horse's back, bothers animals who are not used to it. When you first put the side-saddle on, do the balance girth up just tight enough to keep things in place and lead the horse forwards. Walk him round until he gets used to the feel of it and tighten it gradually.

It is vital that your side-saddle has a safety fitting.

It is easier to make a side-saddle fit a horse than it is to make it fit the rider, as a specialist saddler can do a lot with clever re-flocking. Always make sure that it fits as well as is possible, because a heavy, ill-fitting side-saddle which causes pressure points can do a lot of damage. As far as your comfort and that of the judge is concerned, remember that it is perfectly possible to ride on a saddle that is theoretically too big and often excruciatingly uncomfortable to sit on one that is too small. You might be small and slim, but you cannot guarantee that the judge will be – and it is only too common to hear a judge dismount after the riding section and tell a competitor that the horse was nice, but it was a pity that the saddle spoiled the ride.

For pure showing classes, guidelines for bridles and bits are the same as before; for example, your ladies' hunter would be shown in a hunterweight bridle, either a double or with some kind of pelham. For side-saddle equitation classes, it is correct to use double reins (again, either a double bridle or pelham to suit your horse) if you are riding in a top hat. If you are wearing a bowler, you can use either double reins or a snaffle bridle.

If necessary you can use a small piece of sheepskin under your saddle, but it must be discreet.

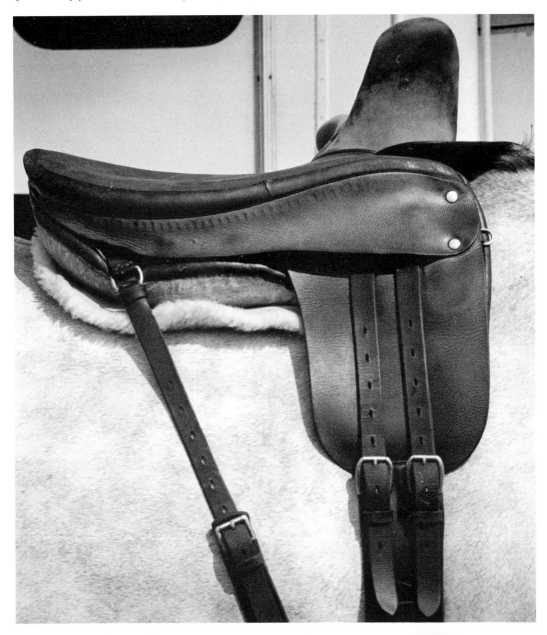

Chapter 13
Final Thoughts

The first year with a new or young horse is a constant learning process for both of you. Every show will reveal something different, whether it is a judge's likes or dislikes or your horse's reaction to distractions such as music.

It is important to learn from all your experiences, the bad ones as well as the good ones. The successful show season is inevitably a well planned one, so buy yourself a large desk diary and look on it as your Bible. It should be used to note down everything from judges' comments to how long it took you to get to a particular show – so at the end of the year, you know which were the best venues and most favourable judges.

If a showground which looks easily accessible on the map turns out to be a nightmare to get to, you might want to find an alternative rather than repeat the experience. Similarly, if you have a grey horse and a particular judge seems to have a pathological dislike of them, it is not worth wasting money on entry fees to show under him or her the following year. Showing is expensive, and your diary can help you save money; after each outing, write down how long it took to get there, how the horse went, judges' comments, fuel costs and anything else that might come in useful for future reference.

Another useful aid to planning the next season is *Horse and Hound* magazine, which publishes a review of the show season each year. This carries the first advertisements for the next season's shows, and by combining it with those carried throughout the year and in the special show issues you can write down in your diary the shows that are open to you against the appropriate dates. You will have to do a bit of lateral thinking – perhaps you are hoping that your horse might be ready to compete at a county show by a certain date, but when you get near the time do not feel quite confident. If this happens, your research will have given you other shows to go to instead.

The show season runs roughly from March through to October. This means that you will need to get all your large stamped addressed envelopes ready to send off by the second or third week in January so that show secretaries can send schedules to you. It is well worth having labels printed with your name and address – you can either do them yourself on a word processor or have them done by a specialist company. It is not expensive, but will save you a lot of time (and time often means money).

Your next purchase should be a large concertina file with at least twelve sections – one per month. As the schedules arrive, you should note the closing date for entries and write on the top of each one in large letters 'Enter by 14 February', or whatever.

As the paperwork mounts up, you will probably start to wish that you had a secretary. You have to make yourself be efficient, even if it does not come naturally! Never leave anything to chance, and take copies of everything from completed entry forms to your horse's height and vaccination certificates. If your horse's original documents ever get lost, you at least have a copy so that new ones can be issued. And if you get to a show and find that your entries have vanished into a black hole, you can present your photocopies to the secretary.

This is the place you are aiming for, at the top of the line. Cosmic winning the lightweight cob class and cob championship at Kent County Show, 1992.

It is important to list all vaccination dates and when they fall due. Enter a reminder in your show diary for a couple of weeks before this to make sure that they can be done in time. It is all too common to see competitors disqualified or prevented from entering a class because their horses' vaccination certificates do not comply with the rules. This inevitably causes a lot of disappointment, especially if someone has spent ages preparing a horse and has travelled a long distance.

The final stage of this blueprint for efficiency is to make a list of all registration numbers on the front of your showing file. This gives an instant cross-reference if a show secretary rings up with a query.

All this sounds as if the showing season is a major campaign. In many ways it is, because whatever level you are competing at, it is a waste of time and money to put in less than your best efforts. The judge sees the final result, but behind that lies all your attention to detail.

If you know you have done your best, then you will enjoy yourself. Showing to win demands a lot of hard work, which hopefully will be helped along by a little luck, but you will get a lot of fun in return.

Useful Addresses

British Show Hack, Cob and Riding Horse Association
Chamberlain House, 88 High Street, Coleshill, Warwickshire B46 3BZ
British Horse Society
British Equestrian Centre, Stoneleigh, Kenilworth, Warwickshire CV8 2LR
British Show Jumping Association
British Equestrian Centre, Stoneleigh, Kenilworth, Warwickshire CV8 2LR
Arab Horse Society
Mrs S. P. Cole, Windsor House, The Square, Ramsbury, Marlborough, Wiltshire SN8 2PL
British Skewbald and Piebald Association
Mrs I. Hutchinson, West Fen House, High Road, Little Downham, Ely,
Cambridgeshire CB6 2TB
British Warmblood Society
Mrs D. Wallin, Moorlands Farm, New Yatt, Witney, Oxfordshire OX8 6TE
Cleveland Bay Horse Society
Mr J. F. Stephenson, York Livestock Centre, Murton, York YO1 3UF
Coloured Horse and Pony Society (CHAPS)
Mrs T. Worman, 38 Lyndhurst Road, Edmonton, London N18 2QA
Irish Draught Horse Society of GB
J. Wood-Roberts, 4th Street, National Agricultural Centre, Stoneleigh,
Warwickshire CV8 2LR
Side-Saddle Association
Mrs M. James, Highbury House, High Street, Wellford, Northampton NN6 7HT

Index